Dreams
&
VISIONS

Dreams & VISIONS

By Edgar Cayce

A.R.E. Press • Virginia Beach • Virginia

A.R.E. Press
215 67th Street
Virginia Beach, VA 23451-2061

ISBN-13: 978-0-87604-546-6 (trade pbk.)

Cover design by Richard Boyle

Contents

Foreword
Who Was Edgar Cayce?

Edgar Cayce (1877–1945) has been called "the sleeping prophet," "the father of holistic medicine," "the miracle man of Virginia Beach," and "the most documented psychic of all time." For forty–three years of his adult life, he had the ability to put himself into some kind of self–induced sleep state by lying down on a couch, closing his eyes, and folding his hands over his stomach. This state of relaxation and meditation enabled him to place his mind in contact with all time and space and to respond to any question he was asked. His responses came to be called "readings" and contain insights so valuable that, even to this day, Cayce's work is known throughout the world. Hundreds of books have explored his amazing psychic gift, and the entire range of Cayce material is accessed by tens of thousands of people daily via the Internet.

Although the vast majority of the Cayce material deals with health and every manner of illness, countless topics were explored by Cayce's psychic talent: dreams, philosophy, intuition, business advice, the Bible, education, child rearing, ancient civilizations, personal spirituality, improving human relationships, and much more. In fact, during Cayce's lifetime he discussed an amazing ten thousand different subjects!

The Cayce legacy presents a body of information so valuable that Edgar Cayce himself might have hesitated to predict its impact on contemporary society. Who could have known that eventually, terms such as *meditation, auras, spiritual growth, reincarnation,* and *holism* would become household words to millions? Edgar Cayce's A.R.E. (the Association for Research and Enlightenment, Inc.) has grown from its humble beginnings to an association with Edgar Cayce Centers in countries around the world. Today the Cayce organizations consist of hundreds of educational activities and outreach programs, children's camps, a multi-million-dollar publishing company, membership benefits and services, volunteer contacts and programs worldwide, massage and health services, prison and prayer outreach programs, conferences and workshops, and affiliated schools (Atlantic University and the Cayce/Reilly School of Massotherapy).

Edgar Cayce was born and reared on a farm near Hopkinsville, Kentucky. He had a normal childhood in many respects. However, he could see the glowing energy patterns that surround individuals. At a very early age he also told his parents that he could see and talk with his grandfather—who was deceased. Later, he developed the ability to sleep on his schoolbooks and retain a photographic memory of their entire contents.

Eventually, he met and fell in love with Gertrude Evans, who would become his wife. Shortly thereafter, he developed a paralysis of the vocal cords and could scarcely speak above a whisper. Everything was tried, but no physician was able to locate a cause. The laryngitis persisted for months. As a last resort, hypnosis was tried. Cayce put himself to sleep and was asked by a specialist to describe the problem. While asleep, he spoke normally, diagnosing the ailment and prescribing a simple treatment. After the recommendations were followed, Edgar Cayce could speak normally for the first time in almost a year! The date was March 31, 1901—that was the first reading.

When it was discovered what had happened, many others began to want help. It was soon learned that Edgar Cayce could put himself into this unconscious state and give readings for anyone—regardless of where he or she was. If the advice was followed, the individual got well. Newspapers throughout the country carried articles about his work, but it wasn't really until Gertrude was stricken with tuberculosis that the readings were brought home to him. Even with medical treatments, she continued to grow worse and was not expected to live. Finally, the doctors said there was nothing more they could do. A reading was given and recommended osteopathy, inhalants, enemas, dietary changes, and prescription medication. The advice was followed and Gertrude returned to perfectly normal health! For decades, the Cayce readings have stood the test of time, research, and extensive study. Further details of Cayce's life and work are explored in such classic books as *There Is a River* (1942) by Thomas Sugrue, *The Sleeping Prophet* (1967) by Jess Stearn, *Many Mansions* (1950) by Gina Cerminara, and *Edgar Cayce: An American Prophet* (2000) by Sidney Kirkpatrick.

Throughout his life, Edgar Cayce claimed no special abilities, nor did he ever consider himself to be some kind of twentieth-century prophet. The readings never offered a set of beliefs that had to be embraced but instead focused on the fact that each person should test in his or her own life the principles presented. Though Cayce himself was a Christian and read the Bible from cover to cover for every year of his life, his work was one that stressed the importance of comparative study among belief systems all over the world. The underlying principle of the readings is the oneness of all life, a tolerance for all people, and a compassion and understanding for every major religion in the world.

An Explanation of Cayce's Discourses

Edgar Cayce dictated all of his discourses from a self-induced trance. A stenographer took his discourses down in shorthand and later typed them. Copies were sent to the person or persons who had requested the psychic reading, and one was put into the files of the organization that built up around Cayce over the years: the Association for Research and Enlightenment (better known as the A.R.E.).

In his normal consciousness, Edgar Cayce spoke with a Southern accent but in the same manner as any other American. However, from the trance state, he spoke in the manner of the King James Bible, using "thees" and "thous." In trance, his syntax was also unusual. He put phrases, clauses, and sentences together in a manner that slows down any reader and requires careful attention in order to be sure of his meaning. This caused his stenographer to adopt some unusual punctuation in order to put into sentence form some of the long, complex thoughts conveyed by Cayce while in trance. Also, many of his discourses are so jampacked with information and insights that it requires that one slow down and read more carefully in order to fully understand what he is intending.

From his trance state, Cayce explained that he got his information from two sources: (1) the inquiring individual's mind, mostly from his or her deeper, subconscious mind and (2) from the Universal Consciousness, the infinite mind within which the entire universe is conscious. He explained that every action and thought of every individual makes an impression upon the Universal Consciousness, an impression that can be psychically read. He correlated this with the Hindu concept of an Akashic Record, which is an ethereal, fourth-dimensional film upon which actions and thoughts are recorded and can be read at any time.

When giving one of his famous health readings, called physical readings, Cayce acted as if he were actually scanning the entire body of the person, from the inside out! He explained that the subconscious mind of everyone contains all of the data on the condition of the physical body it inhabits, and Cayce simply connected with the patient's deeper mind. He could also give the cause of the condition, even if it was from early childhood or from many lifetimes ago in a previous incarnation of the soul. This was knowable because the soul remembers all of its experiences. He explained that deeper portions of the subconscious mind are the mind of the soul, and portions of the subconscious and the soul inhabit the body with the personality.

In life readings and topic readings, Cayce also connected with the subconscious minds of those inquiring as well as the Universal Consciousness.

Occasionally, Cayce would not have the material being requested, and he would say, "We do not have that here." This implied that Cayce's mind was more directed than one might think. He was not open to everything. From trance, he explained that the suggestion given at the beginning of one of his psychic readings so directed his deeper mind and focused it on the task or subject requested that he truly did not have other topics available. However, on a few occasions, he seemed able to shift topics in the middle of a reading.

The typed readings have a standard format. Numbers were used in the place of the name of the person or persons receiving the reading, and a dash system kept track of how many readings the person had received. For example, reading 137-5 was the fifth reading for Mr. [137]. At the top of each reading is the reading number, the date and location, as well as the names or numbers (for privacy) of those in attendance. Occasionally the stenographer would include a note about other conditions, such as the presence of a manuscript that Cayce, in trance, was supposed to view psychically and comment on. In many cases, I left in the entire format of a recorded reading, but sometimes only a paragraph or two were pertinent to our study, and then I only give the reading number.

As I explained, Cayce dictated all of these discourses while he was in trance. In most cases, he spoke in a monotone voice. However, he would sometimes elevate his volume when saying a word or phrase. In these instances, his stenographer usually typed these words with all-capital letters, to give the reader some sense of Cayce's increased volume. These all-capital letters have been changed to italic typeface for readability as well as emphasis. In many cases, these words appear to be rightly accentuated in Cayce's discourses. However, in some cases, it is not clear why he raised his voice.

Another style that the stenographer adopted was to capitalize all of the letters in Cayce's many affirmations (positive-thought or prayer-like passages to be used by the recipient as a tool for focusing or raising consciousness). I have also changed these to upper- and lower-case letters and italicized them. Questions asked of Cayce in these readings have also been italicized for easier reference.

Whenever his stenographer was not sure if she had written down the correct word or thought that she might have missed or misunderstood a word, she inserted suggested words, comments, and explanations in brackets. If she knew of another reading that had similar material or that was being referred to during this reading, she would put the reading number in brackets. Within the text of a reading, all parentheses are asides made by Cayce while in trance, not by his stenographer. She only used brackets with the text of a reading. In the preliminary material, she used parentheses in the normal manner.

A few common abbreviations use in these discourses were: "GD" for Gladys Davis, the primary stenographer, "GC" for Gertrude Cayce, Edgar's wife and the predominant conductor of the readings, MHB for Morton H. Blumenthal, an occasional conductor of the readings, and "EC" for Edgar Cayce.

John Van Auken

An Overview of Edgar Cayce on Dreams and Visions

Perhaps the most striking claim made in the Cayce readings is Cayce's repeated assertion that anyone can do what he did—and we can best begin with our own dreams.

Drawing upon his intimate work with Edgar Cayce, Harman Bro, in his book *Edgar Cayce on Dreams*, states, "The claim that anyone could do, in some measure, what Edgar Cayce did, may well have been the boldest claim he ever made. But he did not let the claim hang in the air. [Cayce] gave people a laboratory where they could investigate the claim for themselves. He urged them to recall and study their dreams. In dreams, he said, people could experience for themselves every important kind of psychic phenomenon, and every level of helpful psychological and religious counsel. What is more, they could, through dreams, learn the laws of these things and undergo a spontaneous and tailored dream-training program in the use of these laws—provided that in their waking life they put to constructive use everything they learned in the dreams."

It was Cayce's avowal that all of the insights and information that arose in his dream, topic, medical, and life readings, including information drawn from past lives and extra-sensory sources, were capable of investigation in the individual's dreams—if the dreamer needed it and could understand it. At the very least, the dreamer who sought it would find direction where to get help, when, and why, both personally and for loved ones.

Cayce viewed consciousness as multi-layered. First is the level of consciousness experienced in everyday awareness. Then comes the level of the subconscious, or what Cayce called the "subconscious forces." According to Elsie Sechrist, in her book *Dreams: Your Magic Mirror*, "[Cayce's] psychic gift enabled him to induce in himself a state of trance or deep sleep that stilled his conscious mind and gave him access to what Jung calls the "collective unconscious"—the universal wisdom of man at its subconscious source. . . . [Cayce] saw the collective or universal subconscious as a vast river of thought flowing through eternity, fed by the sum total of man's mental activity since his beginning. He maintained that this river is accessible to any individual who is prepared to develop his psychic or spiritual faculties with sufficient patience and effort."

As Bro describes, "The dreamer's subconscious—his hidden structures, habits, controls, mechanisms, complexes, formulas—uses the dreamer's own peculiar memory-images and figures of speech to get things done." Here, at the level of the subconscious, the dreamer can easily draw on whatever ESP is possessed as a natural talent or a developed art to get one's bearings on practical matters, and to recover problem-solving items from the distant, the past, or the private.

In Cayce's view, an even deeper source of help is also available. He called it the superconscious, which he described as a higher realm of the subconscious. According to Cayce, there are dreams that can bring into play certain structures of great importance to the dreamer. In these dreams, the dreamer contacts the best, or higher, self—or may even reach to something beyond the self, which Cayce called "the Creative Forces, or God." In Cayce's view, the superconscious is the portion of mind that has retained the memory of God's presence and is man's link with his original spiritual consciousness. These forces can provide the dreamer with boundless information and guidance. As Bro states, "They are . . . the creative currents of the divine itself, moving through human affairs like some great unseen Gulf Stream. In dreams one may reach far beyond his own faculties to tune into these Universal Forces, through his own superconsciousness." Cayce treated the contents of these kinds of dreams with great respect.

Cayce saw the superconscious as the portion of the mind that has retained the memory of God's presence and is man's link with his original spiritual consciousness.

Creating trained dreamers

Before his death in 1945, seventy-seven people received dream interpretations from Edgar Cayce. Altogether, he interpreted 1650 dreams during almost seven hundred readings. The bulk of these readings were for four individuals with whom he worked closely over many years.

The purpose in focusing on these individuals was to create what Cayce called "trained dreamers." His desire was to help them develop the skills needed to guide and interpret their dreams—and thus to use their dreams to help guide their everyday lives and to grow spiritually.

Cayce's greatest challenge in training these dreamers was to get them to rely on themselves, asleep or awake. Bro, who worked directly with Cayce for almost a year, remarks, "He did not seek little Cayce-ites. He wanted capable, self-reliant people, using the talents with which they were endowed, and learning new laws to apply."

Cayce encouraged his dreamers to do more than study dreams and dreaming and to do more than rely on psychics and spiritualists for interpretations or answers. He coached them to interpret and use their own dreams on the problems of everyday life. Through regularly working with their dreams, he pressed them to broaden and deepen their natural psychic, intellectual, financial, leadership, artistic, and healing gifts. He urged them to go into their dreams to access the wisdom and guidance of the Universal Forces.

"After the first few," says Bro, "Cayce never again trained dreamers as such. Instead, he trained people in an explicitly spiritual pilgrimage— one which included dreams but placed still greater weight on meditation, prayer, and daily service to others. Further, he trained people only in groups, where they could daily help one another in study, in love, in mutual intercession, in ways that his major dream subjects rarely knew."

It is thanks to his intensive work with these few individuals that we are able to discern the pattern of laws and principles that govern dreams and our work with them. Through the experiences of these four people, we are able to see how the ability to work with dreams grows, we can witness the kinds of challenges that can be experienced, and we are shown the most effective methods for addressing them.

The purpose of dreams and dreaming

Cayce believed that all phases of humankind's nature are revealed in dreams for the express purpose of directing us to higher and more balanced accomplishments in our physical, mental, and spiritual lives.

According to Cayce, each night we have contact with spiritual and psychic forces through our dreams. Because of this, dreams work to accomplish two things: they work to solve the problems of the dreamer's conscious, waking life, and they work to awaken the dreamer to full stature as a person, to quicken in the dreamer new potentials which are his or hers to claim.

In describing a large part of dreaming as problem solving, Cayce underscored the kind of dreaming that can be called the "incubation" dream. This is the dream that either presents a surprising solution to a problem on which the dreamer has been working or awakens in him a state of consciousness in which the solution he needs springs easily to mind.

Cayce described the rest of meaningful dreaming as quickening the dreamer to his or her own human potentials. Over and over he pointed out how dreams signal to the dreamer that it is time to carry new responsibilities or to develop more mature values or to stretch one's thinking. Such dreams, he said, are not simply solving practical problems—they are helping the dreamer grow.

According to Bro, "[Cayce] described whole cycles of dreams as devoted to developing a new quality in a dreamer: patience, balance, manliness, altruism, humor, reflectiveness, piety. Some of these self-remaking dreams he saw as coming from the efforts of the dreamer's personality to right itself. . . . Other such dreams Cayce saw as spontaneous, healthy presentations, occurring when it was time for a new episode of growth in the dreamer's life."

Everyone dreams—and everyone can remember them

The Cayce readings are clear that anyone who will record dreams in an attitude of prayerful persistence can, in time, bring about a complete restoration of the dream faculty.

As Bro describes, "Those whom Cayce coached had no great difficulty learning to recall dreams, once they set their minds to it. They had to be certain they were ready to confront whatever came forth in dreams, and to do something with it. . . . He was firm with several dreamers that to recall their dreams they should record them—and go back over the records often. . . . Finally, he saw it as important to the process of recalling dreams that dreamers act upon the dreams they recall. The very act of adding consciousness to the subconscious activity which produces the dream will set currents in motion . . . helpful currents to facilitate the recall of the next dreams, and eventually to aid in the interpretation of all dreams. . . . Each of these steps builds recall of dreams. They also build the depth and clarity of the dreams, for they serve to build the dreamer himself."

The four broad kinds of dreams

As an aid to interpreting dreams, Cayce described four broad kinds, or types, of dreams. Sometimes identifying the kind of dream just experienced helps the dreamer begin to interpret its purpose and meaning. While Cayce was clear that some dreams are just nonsense or nightmares, resulting from the body trying to handle troublesome foods or other biological upsets, he said our meaningful dreams fall into these categories or types:

Physical: dreams that provide helpful information about our physical bodies and our health through symbols that may suggest improper diet, a kind of exercise needed, previews of illnesses, and so on. These dreams can even provide specific suggestions for treatment.

Self-revealing: dreams that provide self-knowledge and insight into problems, goals, desires, plans, decisions, relationships, character traits, and so on.

Psychic: dreams that reach out through the windows of telepathy, clairvoyance and precognition to provide insight and information not accessible by our ordinary three-dimensional consciousness.

Spiritual: dreams originating from the dreamer's higher self, dreams flowing from the superconscious mind and the Universal Forces. Cayce often called such dreams "visions."

These four kinds of dreams serve two functions: to solve problems and to aid in spiritual growth.

Interpreting the dreamer, not the dream

The best interpreter of a person's dream is the individual dreamer, since the symbols are one's own. Interpreting dreams, as Cayce described the process, is not just looking up a symbol in a handy dream book and applying it to a dream. Rather, one interprets a *dreamer*, not a dream.

"Study self; study self" was Cayce's first counsel on training to interpret dreams. As Bro says, "If one grasps the dreamer in the dream, one can take the first important step in interpretation: determining which of the two major functions of dreams is to the fore in a particular dream— (a) problem solving and adaptation to external affairs, or (b) awakening and alerting the dreamer to some new potential within him."

Studying dreams and interpreting them is not enough. Bringing dreams into action in everyday life is critical. Cayce called for "application" and included a section on application in every dream reading. While study is a form of application, Cayce had something more concrete in mind. The dreamer must put the insights, tips, and ideas received in dreams into motion in life, trying out the guidance given by experiment. Over and over Cayce counseled his dreamers, Do, do, do.

The lawful patterns of dreaming

Bro points out that the same natural laws or principles that governed Cayce's readings also appear to govern the dreamer's dreams. While these laws were rarely explicitly spelled out in the readings, they can be glimpsed as patterns that are evident in the body of the readings as a whole.

Bro provides a fascinating outline of what he called the "lawful patterns in dreaming." Of particular help are the following:

- "[Cayce] had to be directed to his targets by hypnotic suggestions. For medical counsel he needed the address of the individual who sought aid. For psychological readings he needed the birth date of the individual. And for topical readings, or those on bidden resources, he had to be told both what was sought, and the names and location of those seeking.

"Often those who wanted one type of counsel would request, in the question period following the reading, counsel of another kind. When Cayce was especially keyed up or relating deeply to the person seeking aid, they might get the desired medical information in a business reading, or counsel for a loved one in a dream reading. But more often they would be told, "We do not have this," and instructed to seek a different type of reading.

"Cayce explained to his dreamers that their dream–focus had similar limits. He coached them to set before their minds, by hard study, concentration, and activity, whatever they sought aid upon through dreams. . . . Dreams are limited by the conscious focus of the dreamer."

- "Cayce's readings were limited to the information and guidance which an individual could constructively use; it is the same with dreams, said Cayce. . . . [While unlimited] information [is] available through the subconscious and the other resources, . . . the psyche [protects] its balance by feeding the dreamer limited material. It [operates] by laws of self-regulation."

- "Cayce's health affected his readings. When he was ill he could not give them. . . . Cayce's state of mind [also] affected his readings. When he was distraught and defensive with those about him, he experienced some of the few clear errors in a lifetime of giving readings: once in giving readings on oil wells, and once in giving readings on patients in his hospital. Neither time was a complete miss, but the distortions, as later readings pointed out, were dangerous. . . . His best readings came when he was buoyant, relaxed, humorous, secure. However, he also gave exceptional readings when in keen distress—as when he was twice jailed for giving readings, or when his university collapsed.

"Dreams, too, he said, are conditioned subjectively. He urged his dreamers to get out and play, to take vacations, to balance up their wit and reason, to tease and to laugh and to enjoy children. But he also urged them to note the depth of dreams for the person confronted by death-loss, or by business failure, or by divorce, or by difficult vocational choices—all of which might call forth dreams of such depth and power as to make them 'visions.'"

• "Cayce's readings were affected by what his own trance products described as his relative 'spirituality.' When he was carried away by the ambitions of a treasure hunt, or temptations to seek notoriety with his gift and his considerable lecturing ability, he was reminded to notice how the quality of his readings suffered. On the other hand, when he was regular in his times of prayer and Bible study, as well as in his quiet fishing times, he was reminded to notice that his readings gained in quality, and that he even developed new types of gifts or capacities, both within his readings (for example, producing an entire series on a new subject), or awake (aiding the sick, through prayer).

"Similar factors, his readings said, affect the quality of dreams. When his dreamers drove themselves for money or fame or power, they could see that their dreams brought up these very issues, and then began to deteriorate in clarity and helpfulness. When they were secure in their faith, their prayer times, and in their desire to serve others, they could find new vistas in their dreams—giving them glimpses into the world of the future or the past or the transcendent."

• Frequently, the Cayce source noted that the attitudes of those who sought information and guidance from Cayce affected what they got. Those who sought novelty, exploitation of others, a godlike guarantor for their lives, justification for their past mistakes, or anything but genuine aid and growth, received curt responses, or vague ones, or unexpected lectures on their motives. Those who failed to act on the counsel given them might find future counsel brief or even withheld.

"Gullibility was as readily rejected as cynicism; adulation of Cayce accomplished as little as belittling or envy of him. 'The real miracle,' one reading said, 'occurs in the seeker.'

"Similar factors, he said, govern the extent to which dreamers produce dream information helpful to those about them. Often a dreamer secures facts unavailable to a loved one because of his greater detachment toward the need or problem. Often, too, unconscious telepathy from a brother or sister or child shows dreamers how to reach the other's bad temper, or alcoholic habit, or despairing heart, or overbearing pride."

Improving the usefulness of dreams

To strengthen dream recall and enhance the usefulness of dreams, Cayce emphasized the value of daily contemplation on an affirmation and regularly entering into the deep silence of meditation. Cayce stressed that the spiritually oriented person, whose own intuition is disciplined to a high level, can interpret dreams more exactly than an individual depending solely on his or her own capacity to reason.

But the note which recurred like a silver thread in Cayce's dream readings, whenever he explained to others how to improve their dreaming and their interpretation of dreams, was a familiar one that appeared regularly in his life and medical readings. That note was service.

"For some dreamers, service through dreaming meant literally dreaming for others and giving them aid and counsel," shares Bro. "But such dreamers were few among those who consulted Cayce. Others were encouraged to draw or to write stories based on their dreams. Or to share stock tips secured from their dreams. Or to learn from their dreams the laws of human development, and teach these laws to classes of interested adults. Or to teach others to dream. Or to pray for those presented to them in their dreams. Each one's gifts were different. . . .

"First the dreamer must change and grow. Then he must find a way to share his growth in unassuming service to those closest to him in everyday life. Only then may he find dreams that can occasionally help the leaders in his profession, or his social class, or his school of art, or his reform movement—by helping him to help them.

"It is a law underscored by the failure of the early dreamers that Cayce trained to sustain the high potential which he saw for them, and which they realized at times in both their dreams and their lives. They fell away from one another in their families. This was a blow the straining psyche could not survive, said Cayce, while it was reaching for the heights of dreaming. With his next dreamers he put his first emphasis not on dreaming skill at all, but on loving and producing. There was loving and producing in the family, there was loving and producing in the daily work, there was loving and producing in the gathered fellowship of those who met to study and pray. Only this course—only the course of giving, giving, giving—would keep the flow of dreams clean and ever stronger."

Lawful patterns in dream interpretation

Bro points out that just as there were what he called "lawful processes" that governed every reading Cayce gave and every dream of every dreamer, so there are lawful processes of interpreting dreams. Of particular usefulness are the following:

• "As Cayce took up each dream in a typical dream reading, he first distinguished which levels of the psyche had produced that particular dream. The dreamer can also be taught by his own dreams, he said, to recognize the various levels working within him to produce each dream.

"When a voice speaks in a dream, an aura of feelings and thoughts will show whether the voice is his best self or just his imagination. When a scene from the day flashes across his mind in sleep, he will be shown by nuances whether the scene represents merely worries from the day, or a prologue to helpful comments from the subconscious. When strange and outrageous material appears, his own subconscious will teach him to distinguish which is merely a dream caricature of his outrageous behavior, and which is instead a radical challenge to his being.

"Dreamers should often ask in a dream, or immediately after it, he said, to be shown what part of their mentality has been at work in the dream, and why. Some of Cayce's dreamers were amazed at the colloquy which they were able to follow within them. Others were delighted to be able, they felt, to distinguish their own inner voice from the contribution of discarnates in dreams."

• "In Cayce's view, dreams often carry significant meaning on several levels at once, and should be interpreted accordingly."

- "Part of the art of interpreting dreams, according to Cayce, lies . . . in recognizing symbols with relatively universal meaning. He emphasized the purely personal meaning of much dream contents, from articles of clothing to scenes of war. But he also challenged dreamers to see, in certain poetic and evocative dreams, the presence of symbols which have wide currency in myth and art. Fire often means anger. Light often means insight and help from the divine, as does movement upward. A child often means helpful beginnings, needing further aid from the dreamer. A horse and rider often mean a message from higher realms of consciousness. Pointed objects inserted in openings may be sex symbols—although a key in a lock is more typically unlocking something in the dreamer."

- "One aspect of Cayce's dream interpretation was harder for dreamers to duplicate: the times he predicted their dreams, even the night and time of night. In the strange, wandering world of dreams, this bit of his skill seemed incredible—even allowing for the power of his suggestion upon the dreamer's unconscious. But he said he could do it because he could see factors in the dreamer's psyche which made the dreams inevitable, much as one on a high building could predict the collision of careening cars on separate streets below him. He added that dreamers would also learn to recognize when given dreams were signals of a new theme or series, and to predict for themselves how more would follow—as his dreamers did in lesser degree."

- "In Cayce's view, determining the purpose of a dream is a major step in interpreting it. He explained that the psyche or total being tries to supply whatever the dreamer needs most. If the dreamer needs insight and understanding, it gives him lessons and even discourses. If he needs shaking up, it gives him experiences—beautiful or horrendous. If he needs information, it retrieves the facts for him. Dreams are part of a self-regulating, self-enhancing, self-training program, over which the dreamer's own soul ever presides.

"An important step in interpreting a dream, then, is specifying what it came to accomplish—which the dreamer, according to Cayce, can learn to recognize for himself. A stock discussed by an acquaintance in a dream was a nudge to note and study the stock. But a stock seen in action, in actual figures, or described with instructions by a special kind of voice in his dream, was a signal for the dreamer to act, no longer to study.

"Part of Cayce's training led dreamers to wake up after a vivid dream, review it in their minds so as to recall it later, and then return to sleep with the intention of having the dream interpreted for them—as it not infrequently was, whether by more episodes, or by essay–like passages, or by the voice of an interpreter or 'interviewer,' as one dreamer called it."

Simple Steps to dream interpretation

Kevin Todeschi, in his book *Dream Images and Symbols*, offers this advice on developing the skill of dream interpretation:

"**Step One:** *Write down your dream immediately upon awakening....* Even if you only have the feeling of a good night's sleep, write it down. Let the subconscious mind know that you are serious.

"**Step Two:** *Realize that the feeling you had about the dream is every bit as important as any one possible interpretation.* What is the emotional response you have to the dream, to other characters in the dream, or to the action taking place in the dream? Note the actions, feelings, emotions, and conversations of each of the characters in your dream as well.

"**Step Three:** *Remember that every character in a dream usually represents a part of yourself.* Other people may reflect aspects of your own personality, desires, and fears. Even if the character in the dream is a real person who you know, generally the dream character represents an aspect of yourself in relationship to that person.

"**Step Four:** *Watch for recurring symbols, characters, and emotions in your dreams, and begin a personal dream dictionary.* Write down these symbols and what their importance is to you. As you observe what is going on in your life and then look at a particular dream, you'll begin to have an idea of what individual symbols may mean to you, especially if the symbol appears in later dreams. If the symbol had a voice, what would it be telling you? The symbol won't necessarily mean the same thing to other people, because personal symbols are as individual as the dreamer. For example, dreaming of your teeth falling out may be symbolic of gossip to some people, but an individual who has just been fitted with new dentures may have an entirely different interpretation.

"Step Five: *Practice, practice, practice!* . . . After your dreams have been recorded, make a habit of exploring them a few weeks later. Look for themes, situations, emotions, and symbols that are repetitive. One individual found that her cat, which she dearly loved, frequently appeared in dreams that dealt with personal relationships; another discovered that a watch or a clock was a recurring symbol in precognitive dreams about his personal future. These types of personal insights are only possible with ongoing practice."

Above all—hold to your ideal

"In Cayce's understanding of dreams," says Bro, "a comparison of the dreamer's life with his ideal was occurring in dreams almost every night, however symbolically portrayed, or however small the action examined. . . . In [Cayce's] view, the individual's actions of the previous day, and of the current period of his life, are compared for him each night in sleep with his own deepest ideals. Accordingly, one who awakens grumpy and unrested ought to look into his life, as well as his dreams. And one who awakens in a clear and peaceful frame of mind may be sure that when he recalls his dreams they will not show him in serious inner conflict. . . .

"Further, the remembered dream needs to be used, if possible. . . . The subconscious is like a woodland spring to be dipped out and kept flowing, if it is best used. The dreamer may focus on some portion of the dream that strongly appeals to him, provided it is in keeping with his inmost ideal. For dreams, said Cayce, 'are visions that can be crystallized.' In dreams the real hopes and desires of the person, not idle wishes alone, are given body and force in the individual. . . .

"'Study self, study self,' was Cayce's first counsel on training to interpret dreams. He told people to search out memories, to list their working ideals in columns (physical, mental, spiritual), to decide what they honored in others and to compare this with themselves, to check their self-perception against what others perceived in them. . . . [For] every person who seeks to grow, whether in dreams or awake, must find and assess his own working ideals. . . . Once one clarifies his own deepest ideal, however hard to word and to picture, he must begin lining up his psyche in harmony with it, or his dreams will show him in constant conflict with himself. . . .

"Part of lining up the psyche with its ideal, and ultimately with its Maker, is laying aside fear of past mistakes. Cayce was firm about this, resisting self-condemnation whenever he saw it, and insisting that guilt be replaced with present action. In one of his more startling sayings, he told a dreamer with unpleasant memories of sexual indulgence at the expense of the women in his life that 'no condition is ever lost.' Whatever the failing, even the cruelty, if the dreamer puts his life squarely in the hands of the best he knows, he will find his bitter fruits being turned, over the years, to the wine of understanding for others. What has been one's 'stumbling-block,' he often said, can be made his very 'stepping-stone' towards love and aid to others, because of deep sensitizing action—provided that the psyche is oriented to allow this transmutation to occur."

Seek, and ye shall find; knock, and it shall be opened unto you

Bro leaves us with this final thought:

"One does not need to invent his existence. He has only to 'use what is in hand' and 'the next will be supplied.' For there are two helping forces always at work to guide the unfolding and spending of a human life.

"One force is a person's own original spark of creative energy, a force placed in him at creation, and bearing a potential for love and creativity as great as that of the Creator Itself. The other is a spirit "abroad in the universe" of helpfulness, of unending creativity, kindness, and wisdom. . . . This other force will 'seek its own' within the individual when allowed to do so, and magnify whatever is good within the person.

"In Cayce's view, dreams are of prime importance for the meeting of the ultimate creative force of a person with that other force which ever seeks to help him."

Kristie E. Knutson, Editor

Editor's Note: In this book, the Editor's comments are indicated by the phrase *Editor's Note.*

In addition, you will find the text of some readings repeated in more than one chapter, examples of the richness and depth of the Cayce readings, and how they can be explored and understood in many different contexts.

Cayce's entire collection of readings is available on CD–ROM from the A.R.E., so even though a referenced reading may not be found in this book, they have been included for any future research.

1

●

Cayce on Sleep and Dreams

Reading 3744–5

Editor's Note: The 3744 readings form a series of readings given for the specific purpose of dealing with such metaphysical topics as the nature of the mind; the soul; life after death; and so on.

(Q) What is a dream?

(A) There are many various kinds of manifestations that come to an animate object, or being; that is in the physical plane of man, which the human family term a *dream*.

Some are produced by suggestions as reach the consciousness of the physical, through the various forms and manners as these.

When the physical has laid aside the conscious in that region called sleep, or slumber, when those forces through which the spirit and soul has manifested itself come, and are reenacted before or through or by this soul and spirit force, when such an action is of such a nature as to make or bring back impressions to the conscious mind in the earth or material plane, it is termed a dream.

This may be enacted by those forces that are taken into the system, and in the action of digestion that takes place under the guidance of subconscious forces, become a part of that force through which the spirit and soul of that entity passed at such time. Such manifestations are termed or called nightmares, or the abnormal manifestations on the physical plane of these forces.

In the normal force of dreams are enacted those forces that may be the fore-shadow of condition, with the comparison by soul and spirit forces of the condition in *various spheres* through which this soul and spirit of the given entity has passed in its evolution to the present sphere. In this age, at present, 1923, there is not sufficient credence given dreams; for the best development of the human family is to give the greater increase in knowledge of the subconscious, soul or spirit world. This is a *dream*.

(Q) *How should dreams be interpreted?*

(A) Depending upon the physical condition of the entity and that which produces or brings the dream to that body's forces.

The better definition of how the interpretation may be best is this: Correlate those Truths that are enacted in each and every dream that becomes a part of this, or the entity of the individual, and use such to the better developing, ever remembering develop means going toward the higher forces, or the Creator.

Reading 853–8

(Q) *Do I actually leave my body at times, as has been indicated, and go to different places?*

(A) You do.

(Q) *For what purpose, and how can I develop and use this power constructively?*

(A) Just as has been given as to how to enter into meditation. Each and every soul leaves the body as it rests in sleep.

As to how this may be used constructively—this would be like answering how could one use one's voice for constructive purposes. It is of a same or of a similar import, you see; that is, it is a faculty, it is an experience, it is a development of the self as related to spiritual things, material things, mental things.

Then as to the application of self in those directions for a development of same—it depends upon what is the purpose, what is the desire. Is it purely material? Is it in that attitude, "If or when I am in such and such a position I can perform this or that"? If so, then such expressions are only excuses within self—in any phase of an experience.

For as He has given, it is here a little, there a little—Use that you have in hand today, *now*, and when your abilities and activities are such that you may be entrusted with other faculties, other developments, other experiences, they are a part of self.

As to how it may be used: Study to show thyself approved unto God, a workman not ashamed of that you think, of that you do, or of your acts; keeping self unspotted from your own consciousness of your ideal; having the courage to dare to do that you know is in keeping with God's will.

Reading 294-15

As we see, all visions and dreams are given for the benefit of the individual, would they but interpret them correctly, for we find that visions, or dreams, in whatever character they may come, are the reflection, either of the physical condition, with apparitions with same, or of the subconscious, with the conditions relating to the physical body and its action, either through mental or through the elements of the spiritual entity, or a projection from the spiritual forces to the subconscious of the individual, and happy may he be that is able to say they have been spoken to through the dream or vision.

Reading 903-5

Dreams as come to a body are of different nature and character, dependent upon through what channel these are brought to the physical consciousness of the body. All are not brought entirely to the sensuous consciousness; yet often—even though of experience of subconscious mind—may influence an individual as to the trend or bend of the mental action of the mind for quite a period, or until something else may fill the consciousness. Consciousness, in this sense, not wholly that known in the physical as sensuous consciousness; rather an innate consciousness than a sensuous consciousness. Rather an attribute, then, under such conditions, of the subconscious than of the conscious mind.

In the dream—some may be as dreams of a conscious or the subconscious mind, or a correlation of each—or these may be visions of projection of subconsciousness of other minds acting with the subconscious forces of an individual. These—or this character—are always visions. Well that one differentiate between a vision and a dream, or a purely physical reaction.

Reading 140-6

The dreams are that, that the entity may gain the more perfect understanding and knowledge of those forces that go to make up the real existence—what it's all about and what it's good for—if the entity would but comprehend the conditions being manifest before same. For as the visions in dream are presented, the inner forces of the entity, in no uncertain way, are presenting emblematical conditions to the entity for its study and for its good, see?

Reading 341-18

The dreams come in that way and manner as we have given, and may be used in the way of the entity's development, in the entity's gaining that of how the subconscious weighs with the conscious forces of the entity, when these apply to action, and may be acted upon by the physical body.

Reading 538-13

The dreams as come to the body give that of the lessons that, were same applied correctly in the life of the individual, there will come the more perfect understanding, and those pleasures and joys as would be derived in living that life.

Reading 137-24

The dreams as we see that come to this body are those injunctions to the body of how the forces as may be applied through the entity are presented, and the entity may use same in that manner as has been given. For through these the entity may more perfectly understand those laws as pertain to the manifestations of the psychic forces in the material world. And many of these, we see, pertain to the physical conditions through which entity may see that manifestation in a physical manner, though the conditions are presented at times in emblematical form. Then study well, knowing that the entrance into same gives the more perfect way of understanding—yet must not be turned from.

Reading 39-3

With dreams and visions as come to individual, these are of various classes and groups, and are the emanations from the conscious, subconscious, or superconscious, or the combination and correlation of each, depending upon the individual and the personal development of the individual, and are to be used in the lives of such for the betterment of such individual.

Reading 136-45

Yes, we have the body, the enquiring mind, [136]. This we have had here before. The dreams, the visions, the impressions as are gained in experiences through the subconscious forces, are giving to the entity those lessons, as may be applied in the physical body, the physical mind, and in the material manner, as has been outlined for the body. The lessons as are being gained by same are as the truths that come by the entity making itself in an attunement and an at-onement with those universal forces, into which the body-conscious mind enters when in the somnambulistic state, or in sleep: for the subconscious force operates on.

Use same, then, and apply same for the better conditions, the better understanding of life and life's purposes, and of those conditions through which the entity passes. For each experience *applied* is a development for the entity. Without an application of the experience is to act in that way that brings condemnation, or a mis-application of the advantages as may be gained by knowledge.

Reading 5754-1

Editor's Note: This is the first of three readings in a series on the nature of sleep.]

GC: You will please outline clearly and comprehensively the material which should be presented to the general public in explaining just what occurs in the conscious, subconscious and spiritual forces of an entity while in the state known as sleep. Please answer the questions which will be asked regarding this:

EC: Yes. While there has been a great deal written and spoken regarding experiences of individuals in that state called sleep, there has only recently been the attempt to control or form any definite idea of what produces conditions in the unconscious, subconscious, or subliminal or subnormal mind, by attempts to produce a character—or to determine that which produces the character—of dream as had by an individual or entity. Such experiments may determine for some minds questions respecting the claim of some psychiatrist or psycho-analyst and through such experiments refute or determine the value of such in the study of certain character of mental disturbances in individuals; yet little of this may be called true analysis of what happens to the body, either physical, mental, subconscious or spiritual, when it loses itself in such repose. To be sure, there are certain definite conditions that take place respecting the physical, the conscious, and the subconscious, as well as spiritual forces of a body.

So, in analyzing such a state for a comprehensive understanding, all things pertaining to these various factors must be considered.

First, we would say, sleep is a shadow of, that intermission in earth's experiences of, that state called death; for the physical consciousness becomes unaware of existent conditions, save as are determined by the attributes of the physical that partake of the attributes of the imaginative or the subconscious and unconscious forces of that same body; that is, in a normal sleep (physical standpoint we are reasoning now) the *senses* are on guard, as it were, so that the auditory forces are those that are the more sensitive.

The auditory sense being of the attributes or senses that are more universal in aspect, when matter in its evolution has become aware of itself being capable of taking from that about itself to sustain itself in its present state. That is as of the lowest to the highest of animate objects or beings. From the lowest of evolution to the highest, or to man.

So, then, we find that there are left what is ordinarily known as four other attributes that are acting independently and coordinatingly in *awareness* for a physical body to be conscious. These, in the state of sleep or repose, or rest, or exhaustion, or induced by any influence from the outside, have become *unaware* of that which is taking place about the object so resting.

Then, there is the effect that is had upon the body as to what becomes, then, more aware to those attributes of the body that are not aware of that existent about them, or it. The organs that are of that portion known as the inactive, or not necessary for conscious movement, keep right on with their functioning—as the pulsations, the heart beat, the assimilating and excretory system, keep right on functioning; yet there are periods during such a rest when even the heart, the circulation, may be said to be at rest. What, then, *is* that that is not in action during such period? That known as the sense of perception as related to the physical brain. Hence it may be truly said, by the analogy of that given, that the auditory sense is sub-divided, and there is the act of hearing by feeling, the act of hearing by the sense of smell, the act of hearing by *all* the senses that are independent of the brain centers themselves, but are rather of the lymph centers—or throughout the entire sympathetic system is such an accord as to be *more* aware, *more* acute, even though the body-physical and brain-physical *is* at repose, or *unaware.*

Of what, then, does this sixth sense partake, that has to do so much with the entity's activities by those actions that may be brought about by that passing within the sense *range* of an entity when in repose, that may be called—in their various considerations or phases—experiences of *something* within that entity, as a dream—that may be either in toto to that which is to happen, is happening, or may be only presented in some form that is emblematical—to the body or those that would interpret such.

These, then—or this, then—the sixth sense, as it may be termed for consideration here, partakes of the *accompanying* entity that is ever on guard before the throne of the Creator itself, and is that that may be trained or submerged, or left to its *own* initiative until it makes either war *with* the self in some manner of expression—which must show itself in a material world as in dis-ease, or disease, or temper, or that we call the blues, or the grouches, or any form that may receive either in the waking state or in the sleep state, that has *enabled* the brain in its activity to become so changed or altered as to respond much in the manner as does a string tuned that vibrates to certain sound in the manner in which it is strung or played upon.

Then we find, this sense that governs such is that as may be known as the other self of the entity, or individual. Hence we find there must be some definite line that may be taken by that other self, and much that then has been accorded—or recorded—as to that which may produce certain given effects in the minds or bodies (not the minds, to be sure, for its active forces are upon that outside of that in which the mind, as ordinarily known, or the brain centers themselves, functions), but—as may be seen by all such experimentation, these may be produced—the same effect—upon the same individual, but they do not produce the same effect upon a different individual in the same environment or under the same circumstance. Then, this should lead one to know, to understand, that there is a *definite* connection between that we have chosen to term the sixth sense, or acting through the auditory forces of the body-physical, and the other self within self.

In purely physical, we find in sleep the body is *relaxed*—and there is little or no tautness within same, and those activities that function through the organs that are under the supervision of the sub-conscious or unconscious self, through the involuntary activities of an organism that has been set in motion by that impulse it has received from its first germ cell force, and its activity by the union *of* those forces that have been impelled or acted upon by that it has fed upon in all its efforts and activities that come, then it may be seen that these may be shown by due consideration—that the same body fed upon *meats*, and for a period—then the same body fed upon only herbs and fruits—would *not* have the same character or activity of the other self in its relationship to that as would be experienced by the other self in its activity through that called the dream self.

We are through for the moment—present.

Reading 5754-2

EC: Now, with that as has just been given, that there is an active force within each individual that functions in the manner of a sense when the body-physical is in sleep, repose or rest, we would then outline as to what are the functions of this we have chosen to call a sixth sense.

What relation does it bear with the normal physical recognized five senses of a physical-aware body? If these are active, what relation do they bear to this sixth sense?

Many words have been used in attempting to describe what the spiritual entity of a body is, and what relations this spirit or soul bears with or to the active forces within a physical normal body. Some have chosen to call this the cosmic body, and the cosmic body as a sense in the universal consciousness, or that portion of same that is a part of, or that body with which the individual, or man, is clothed in his advent into the material plane.

These are correct in many respects, yet by their very classification, or by calling them by names to designate their faculties or functionings, have been limited in many respects.

But what relation has this sixth sense (as has been termed in this presented) with this *soul* body, this cosmic consciousness? What relation has it with the faculties and functionings of the normal physical mind? Which must be trained? The sixth sense? or must the body be trained in its other functionings to the dictates of the sixth sense?

In that as presented, we find this has been termed, that this ability or this functioning—that is so active when physical consciousness is laid aside—or, as has been termed by some poet, when the body rests in the arms of Morpheus—is nearer possibly to that as may be understandable by or to many; for, as given, this activity—as is seen—of a mind, or an attribute of the mind in physical activity—*leaves* a *definite* impression. Upon what? The mental activities of the body, or upon the subconscious portion of the body (which, it has been termed that, it never forgets), upon the spiritual essence of the body, or upon the soul itself? These are questions, not statements!

In understanding, then, let's present illustrations as a pattern, that there may be comprehension of that which is being presented:

The activity, or this sixth sense activity, is the activating power or force of the other self. What other self? That which has been builded by the entity or body, or soul, through its experiences as a whole in the material and cosmic world, see? or is as a faculty of the soul-body itself. Hence, as the illustration given, does the subconscious make aware to this active force when the body is at rest, or this sixth sense, some action on the part of self or another that is in disagreement with that which has been builded by that other self, then *this* is the warring of conditions or emotions within an individual. Hence we may find that an individual may from sorrow *sleep* and wake with a feeling of elation. What has taken place? We possibly may then understand what we are speaking of. There has been, and ever when the physical consciousness is at rest, the other self communes with the *soul* of the body, see? or it goes *out* into that realm of experience in the relationships of all experiences of that entity that may have been throughout the *eons* of time, or in correlating *with* that as it, that entity, *has* accepted as its criterion or standard of judgments, or justice, within its sphere of activity.

Hence through such an association in sleep there may have come that peace, that understanding, that is accorded by that which has been correlated through that passage of the selves of a body in sleep. Hence we find the more spiritual-minded individuals are the more easily pacified, at peace, harmony, in normal active state as well as in sleep. Why? They have set before themselves (Now we are speaking of one individual!) that that *is* a criterion that may be wholly relied upon, for that from which an entity or soul sprang is its *concept*, its awareness of, the divine or creative forces within their experience. Hence they that have named the Name of the Son have put their trust in Him. He their standard, their model, their hope, their activity. Hence we see how that the action through such sleep, or such quieting as to enter the silence— What do we mean by entering the silence? Entering the presence of that which *is* the criterion of the selves of an entity!

On the other hand oft we find one may retire with a feeling of elation, or peace, and awaken with a feeling of depression, of aloofness, of being alone, of being without hope, or of fear entering, and the *body-physical* awakes with that depression that manifests itself as of low spirits, as is termed, or of coldness, gooseflesh over the body, in expressions of the forces. What has taken place? A comparison in that "arms of Morpheus", in that silence, in that relationship of the physical self being unawares of those comparisons between the soul and its experiences of that period with the experiences of itself throughout the ages, and the experience may not have been remembered as a dream—but it lives *on*—and on, and must find its expression in the relationships of all it has experienced in whatever sphere of activity it may have found itself.

Hence we find oft individual circumstances of where a spiritual-minded individual in the material plane (that is, to outward appearances of individuals so viewing same) suffering oft under pain, sickness, sorrow, and the like. What takes place? The experiences of the soul are meeting that which it has merited, for the clarification for the associations of itself with that whatever has been set as its ideal. If one has set self in array against that of love as manifested by the Creator, in its activity brought into material plane, then there *must* be a continual—continual—*warring* of those elements. By the comparison we may find, then, how it was that, that energy of creation manifested in the Son—by the activities of the Son in the material plane, could say "He sleeps", while to the outward eye it was death; for He *was*—and *is*—and ever will be—Life and Death in one; for as we find ourselves *in* His presence, that we have builded in the soul makes for that condemnation or that pleasing of the presence of that in His presence. So, my son, let thine lights be in Him, for these are the *manners* through which all may come to an understanding of the activities; for, as was given, "I was in the Spirit on the Lord's day." "I was caught up to the seventh heaven. Whether I was in the body or out of the body I cannot tell." What was taking place? The subjugation of the physical attributes in accord and attune with its infinite force as set as its ideal brought to that soul, "Well done, thou good and faithful servant, enter into the joys of thy Lord." "He that would be the greatest among you—" Not as the Gentiles, not as the heathen, not as the scribes or Pharisees, but "He that would be the greatest will be the *servant* of all."

What, then, has this to do—you ask—with the subject of sleep? Sleep—that period when the soul takes stock of that it has acted upon during one rest period to another, making or drawing—as it were—the comparisons that make for Life itself in its *essence*, as for harmony, peace, joy, love, long-suffering, patience, brotherly love, kindness—these are the fruits of the Spirit. Hate, harsh words, unkind thoughts, oppressions and the like, these are the fruits of the evil forces, or Satan and the soul either abhors that it has passed, or enters into the joy of its Lord. Hence we see the activities of same. This an *essence* of that which is intuitive in the active forces. Why should this be so in one portion, or one part of a body, rather than another? How received woman her awareness?

Through the sleep of the man! Hence *intuition* is an attribute of that made aware through the suppression of those forces from that from which it sprang, yet endowed *with* all of those abilities and forces of its Maker that made for same its activity in an *aware* world, or—if we choose to term it such—a three dimensional world, a *material* world, where its beings must see a materialization to become aware of its existence in that plane; yet all are aware that the essence of Life itself as the air that is breathed—carries those elements that are not aware consciously of any existence to the body, yet the body subsists, lives upon such. In sleep all things become possible, as one finds self flying through space, lifting, or being chased, or what not, by those very things that make for a comparison of that which has been builded by the very soul of the body itself.

What, then, is the sixth sense? Not the soul, not the conscious mind, not the subconscious mind, not intuition alone, not any of those cosmic forces—but the very force or activity of the soul in its experience through *whatever* has been the experience of that soul itself. See? The same as we would say, is the mind of the body the body? No! Is the sixth sense, then, the soul? No! No more than the mind is the body! for the soul is the *body* of, or the spiritual essence of, an entity manifested in this material plane.

We are through for the present.

Reading 5754-3

EC: Yes, we have that which has been given here. Now, as we have that condition that exists with the body and this functioning, or this sense, or this ability of sleep and sense, or a sixth sense, just what, how, may this knowledge be used to advantage for an individual's development towards that it would attain?

As to how it may be used, then, depends upon what is the ideal of that individual; for, as has been so well pointed out in Holy Writ, if the ideal of the individual is lost, then the abilities for that faculty or that sense of an individual to contact the spiritual forces are gradually lost, or barriers are builded that prevent this from being a sensing of the nearness of an individual to a spiritual development.

As to those who are nearer the spiritual realm, their visions, dreams, and the like, are more often—and are more often retained by the individual; for, as is seen as a first law, it is self-preservation. Then self rarely desires to condemn self, save when the selves are warring one with another, as are the elements within a body when eating of that which produces what is termed a nightmare—they are warring with the senses of the body, and partake either of those things that make afraid, or produce visions of the nature as partaking of the elements that are taken within the system, and active within same itself. These may be given as examples of what it is all about.

Then, how may this be used to develop a body in its relationship to the material, the mental, and the spiritual forces?

Whether the body desires or not, in sleep the consciousness physically is laid aside. As to what will be that it will seek, depends upon what has been builded as that it would associate itself with, physically, mentally, spiritually, and the closer the association in the mental mind in the physical forces, in the physical attributes, are with spiritual elements, then—as has been seen by even those attempting to produce a certain character of vision or dream—these follow much in that; for another law that is universal becomes active! Like begets like! That which is sown in honor is reaped in glory. That which is sown in corruption cannot be reaped in glory; and the likings are associations that are the companions of that which has been builded; for such experiences as dreams, visions and the like, are but the *activities* in the unseen world of the real self of an entity.

Ready for questions.

(Q) *How may one train the sixth sense?*

(A) This has just been given; that which is constantly associated in the mental visioning in the imaginative forces, that which is constantly associated with the senses of the body, that will it develop toward. What is that which is and may be sought? When under stress *many* an individual—There are *no* individuals who haven't at *some time* been warned as respecting that that may arise in their daily or physical experience! Have they heeded? Do they heed to that as may be given as advice? No! It must be experienced!

(Q) *How may one be constantly guided by the accompanying entity on guard at the Throne?*

(A) It is there! It's as to whether they desire or not! It doesn't leave but
is the active force? As to its ability to *sense* the variations in the experiences that are seen, is as has been given in the illustration—"As to
whether in the body or out of the body, I cannot tell." Hence this sense
is that ability of the entity to associate its physical, mental or spiritual
self to that realm that it, the entity, or the mind of the soul, seeks for its
association during such periods—see? This might confuse some, for—as
has been given—the subconscious and the abnormal, or the unconscious conscious, is the mind of the soul; that is, the sense that this is
used, as being that subconscious or subliminal self that is on guard ever
with the Throne itself; for has it not been said, "He has given his angels
charge concerning thee, lest at any time thou dashest thy foot against a
stone?" Have you heeded? Then He is near. Have you disregarded? He
has withdrawn to thine own self, see? That self that has been builded,
that that is as the companion, that must be presented—that *is* presented—*is* before the Throne itself! *Consciousness*—[physical] consciousness—see—man seeks this for his *own* diversion. In the sleep [the soul]
seeks the *real* diversion, or the *real* activity of self.

(Q) *What governs the experiences of the astral body while in the fourth dimensional plane during sleep?*

(A) This is, as has been given, that upon which it has fed. That which
it has builded; that which it seeks; that which the mental mind, the
subconscious mind, the subliminal mind, *seeks!* That governs. Then we
come to an understanding of that, "He that would find must seek." In
the physical or material this we understand. That is a pattern of the
subliminal or the spiritual self.

(Q) *What state or trend of development is indicated if an individual does not remember dreams?*

(A) The negligence of its associations, both physical, mental and spiritual. Indicates a very negligible personage!

(Q) *Does one dream continually but simply fail to remember consciously?*

(A) Continues an association or withdraws from that which is its right,
or its ability to associate! There is no difference in the unseen world to
that that is visible, save in the unseen so much greater expanse or space
may be covered! Does one always desire to associate itself with others?
Do individuals always seek companionship in this or that period of

their experiences in each day? Do they withdraw themselves from? That desire lies or carries on! See? It's a *natural* experience! It's *not* an unnatural! Don't seek for unnatural or supernatural! It is the natural—it is nature—it is God's activity! His associations with man. His *desire* to make for man a way for an understanding! Is there seen or understood fully that illustration that was given of the Son of man, that while those in the ship were afraid because of the elements the Master of the sea, of the elements, slept? What associations may there have been with that sleep? Was it a natural withdrawing? Yet when spoken to, the sea and the winds obeyed His voice. Thou may do even as He, wilt thou make thineself aware—whether that awareness through the ability of those forces within self to communicate with, understand, those elements of the spiritual life *in* the conscious and unconscious, these be one!

(Q) *Is it possible for a conscious mind to dream while the astral or spirit body is absent?*

(A) There may be dreams—(This is a division here) A conscious mind, while the body is absent, is as one's ability to divide self and do two things at once, as is seen by the activities of the mental mind.

The ability to read music and play is using different faculties of the same mind. Different portions of the same consciousness. Then, for one faculty to function while another is functioning in a different direction is not only possible but probable, dependent upon the ability of the individual to concentrate, or to centralize in their various places those functionings that are manifest of the spiritual forces in the material plane. *Beautiful*, isn't it?

(Q) *What connection is there between the physical or conscious mind and the spiritual body during sleep or during an astral experience?*

(A) It's as has been given, that *sensing!* With what? That separate sense, or the ability of sleep, that makes for acuteness with those forces in the physical being that are manifest in everything animate. As the unfolding of the rose, the quickening in the womb, of the grain as it buds forth, the awakening in all nature of that which has been set by the divine forces, to make the awareness of its presence in *matter*, or material things.

We are through for the present.

2

●

Receiving Life Guidance in Dreams

Editor's Note: The following is information on understanding symbols.

Hugh Lynn Cayce, in the book *Dreams: The Language of the Unconscious*, states, "The following symbols and their brief interpretation from the Edgar Cayce readings should not be used like a dream book to look up the meaning of your dream symbols. They are given here to fill out the pattern of this large category dealing with understanding self. A few words of a foreign language can be confusing and inadequate. Each person should study the language of his own unconscious, realizing that even the symbols that seem most obvious are frequently used in one's own dreams in a very individual manner."

Water—Source of life, spirit, unconscious
Boat—Voyage of life
Explosion—Turmoils
Fire—Wrath, cleansing, destroying
A person—Represents what the dreamer feels toward that person
Clothing—Way one appears to others
Animals—Represent some phase of self, according to what one feels
    about the animal seen. In this area especially the universal,
    historical, and racial quality of meanings must be considered.

For example, the bull, sexless human figure, lion and eagle may for many persons symbolize the four lower vital centers of the body: the sex glands, cells of leydig, adrenals, and thymus, in that order. The snake is both a wisdom symbol and a sex symbol, associated with the kundalini. When raised to the higher centers in the head it becomes the wisdom symbol.

Fish—Christ, Christian, spiritual food

Dead leaves—body drosses

Mud, mire, tangled weeds—That needing cleansing

Naked—open to criticism, exposed

Reading 294–40

(Q) Are we to understand from this [reading 294-39] that every dream that is had by EC in Virginia Beach should be interpreted through the psychic forces?

(A) Those that make such an impression on the conscious forces as to become a portion of the mental activities of the mind, these should be interpreted. Those that are caused by conditions produced by foods taken, that are of a physical nature, need not be, see?

(Q) How may he distinguish these, one from the other?

(A) One is well remembered, the other as a nightmare, see? or worry, without any specific heads, tails or points, see?

Editor's Note: Dreams that focus on the physical body.

Reading 137–61

(Q) Feb. 18 or 19, 1926. Had my tonsils taken out.

(A) With the condition as exists in the body in the physical way and manner, again we find the physical-mental attempting to present to the entity those relations with existent conditions, or something to occur, see? Yet we do not find the relation as presented with the subconscious forces as of an action to take place in a definite time, or in a definite way and manner. Rather, then, should the entity be warned to care. Be sure that such conditions do not arise and have the troubles with same as has been experienced in times back, physically, see?

Reading 137–60

(Q) Wednesday night, Jan. 20, or Thursday morning, Jan. 21, 1926. I wanted a large cup of coffee, but I was given a demitasse (a small cup).

(A) Necessary, then, that the physical conditions of the body, as is seen, that the subconscious reasons the more perfect for the condition of the entity, that not too heavy, not too much stimulation in this character of caffeine for the body be taken therein.

Reading 137–66

(Q) Evening of March 6, 1926. While asleep it seemed I tried to awaken but could not. As I fought to wake up the blood seemed to rush to my head and also gave me a headache. I then did wake up, thinking of making fudge.

(A) There is much more of this dream. There is seen and presented to the entity, in this portion as is retained by the consciousness, as is seen here, how that the subconscious force of the entity warning the entity as to the conditions of the physical forces, and that *through* which the condition becomes existent. That is, as is seen, the subconscious not able to wake—the change or flow of blood—headache, and with the headache, and the awakening desiring, physically, fudge. The mental forces are not subjugated sufficient as relating to desires (flesh) for the needs of the body. An over amount of those properties such as fudge *hinders* the circulation.

Reading 900–234

(Q) [[137]'s dreams]: Wednesday Night, May 5, or Thursday Morning, May 6, 1926. I was at what seemed to be a family party. We were eating refreshments when Edward Blum and someone started to fight. Hot words led to a fist fight and I finally separated them.

(A) In this there is presented to the entity that warning as to the diets in the physical forces of the body; for, as has been given that the entity should be warned as respecting that that is taken in the system, especially in the way of sweets and of those things that overload the weakened condition in the red blood supply of the body, as there is seen in the vision, the entity attempts and seems unable at first, yet overcomes the conditions, same as may be seen in the physical manner that the body will, through will's force of the physical body, overcome those conditions that would be detrimental to the best interests of the body, mentally and physically.

As is seen in the special individual, as that individual represents in the mental mind of the body, [137], certain conditions in the physical or moral plane, then those that are represented by same are those that should be warned of, for, as is seen, there has been given that the entity should take some stimulants occasionally for the weakness in the physical forces of the body, but of a specific nature, and that will have certain specific conditions produced by same. Then, in taking the sweets in certain forms, as are seen, these produce a different character of alcohol within the body itself. This nature, or this character of same, with the condition, proving then detrimental. Thence, be warned of the physical conditions of the body, especially as the warm weather begins, see?

Reading 136–21 12/2/25

(Q) *Sunday morning, November 29. I was going into swim from a rickety platform—very unsubstantial in its structure. As I jumped in or tried to dive in, I made a belly whapper—i.e. landed on my stomach—it hurt.*

(A) In this we find there is brought to the conscious mind in an emblematical manner and form, through physical conditions existent in the body, that which may be used as the lesson for the entity, see? For as the pain in the inmost portion of the torso gives rise to the emblematical condition presented, the entering the water, the desire to swim, to dive, the entering into those conditions as regard to motherhood—and as the body finds self in the attitude ready for that, the physical conditions or structure in which the body has kept self is not prepared in the manner as would bring the better conditions for the condition of that office at this time, see? And as this will soon occur, the body should take cognizance and be more sure of that position by and in self for this greatest of offices given to the sex—woman. [2/26/25 She had miscarriage.] [GD's note: Her son was born 16 months later on 4/4/27.]

Reading 136–29

(Q) *The family, including [900], were quarreling over my mother [139] and her health and what should or should not be done. The Voice: "Listen and heed two doctors first: Dr. Eldsberge & second Dr.—" The name of the second doctor forgotten.*

Who is this second doctor to be heeded?

(A) (interrupting) The Great Physician.

(Q) (continuing) And just exactly what event is referred to here?

(A) . . . As is given, heed physically in that way as given by the physician in charge, for this is the mechanical end; yet the One as forgotten, one as unheeded, unheralded, gives the greater promise and the supplying force to the mechanical, and through the spirit elements supplies that necessary for the curative forces in each and every individual.

Then the lesson: Though same may be viewed from the material end, yet within that force which is supplied through the divine forces as are manifest, is that ever ready influence in the lives of all, if all would heed.

Reading 379-9

(Q) What is the cause and effects of the sweats and nightmare that I had on Sunday night, May 16th?

(A) Poor circulation, disturbance between the purely mental–physical forces and the imaginative or spiritual forces, with the general debilitations—see? The attempting, as it were, of coordination.

Reading 136-54

(Q) Night of December 28, or morning of 29, 1926. I was in India and many streams seemed to run into the one pool. I jumped in one and swam and said to [900]: See, you said it would hurt me to do this—harm my pregnant condition, but it has not at all.

(A) Again we find a different phase of conditions presented through the mentality of the individual regarding conditions in which the body might indulge, and questioning conditions arise in the minds of others as to whether the entity should or should not indulge. And, as is seen, India represents to the mentality of the entity a state of condition. Water represents another element of beginning or sources of all force. The entering into that of all source of force brings to the entity the knowledge of safety, see? Then, the lesson as may be gained may be more than twofold—that is, that the presented conditions are that, when the entity is at an at–oneness with the source of force, the entity's actions with same are nearer in keeping with the universal forces, see?

Hence conditions so applied in purpose, in intent, and in the full knowledge of the at-oneness of force brings to this entity, to other entities, that security in the all-powerful forces of universal expression or universal manifestation in the material plane.

Hence many conditions are detrimental to an entity because the entity thinks they will be, or has been told they will be, see? while in self, if known that they will not be—will not be, see? Referring to every element wherein the entity may take thought, whether as to trip, or whether as to any conditions in which the entity would indulge—that is, would the entity be in whole at-oneness with the divine purposes as would be set forth by the conditions as are existent in every element, these would not be detrimental—but rather beneficial, see? This does not indicate that one may attempt to defeat any of the natural *laws* as are set forth, for compliance with the law is to become the law—not at variance with the law!

Editor's Note: Dreams on life lessons.

Reading 136-7

(Q) *June 25, 1925, at home in Deal. Dreamed of teeth and my sister-in-law, [140], who said to me, "I'll have to get all false teeth."*

(A) This, as we see, is again a correlating of physical conditions, through the subconscious projection in an emblematical form and manner, indicating that there will come sharp words between the two individuals seen. The lesson: Knowing that such will occur and that there perhaps would be exception taken at something that might be said, do not allow same to make a difference in conditions that should exist between the two.

Reading 137-54

(Q) *Something about not dreaming properly. That is, I was making myself sick.*

(A) Rather that as is presented (of making the self sick), making self not taking, not accepting, not building, on dreams or visions, or that as being presented. Then to the entity, there is as this: Again and again the entity catches, through experience, through dream, through vision, those conditions that, builded into the full consciousness of self, with that decided stand as within self concerning those as are seen, would bring the greater peace, joy, happiness, understanding, and in the physical build the greater strength, be the greater help in all times of need. Then take same. Then apply same, that the light, as may be given to others through this entity, may shine; not as one reflected, but as from one whom is giving of self in the way of being the reflection of *self* in that light.

Reading 1968-10

(Q) *What is meant in my life reading by the statement that I would have imposing dreams and how can I best interpret them to be helpful to me in the present?*

(A) These have come, these may come. Ye interpret them in thyself. Not by dream book, not by what others say, but dreams are presented in symbols, in signs. Oft they may be as opposite that which is presented to the body which has been in some of those indicated that bring warnings, blessings. Then keep thyself pure in mind and body. For the Lord's are oft spoken in dreams, in visions. For He is the same yesterday, today and forever. Be not unmindful that there is the manner of life ye live so that ye merit this or that experience.

Reading 106-6

GC: You will have before you the body of [106], and the dreams this body had in her apartment . . . , New York City. The first dream on Tuesday night, March 10th, or early Wednesday morning, March 11th, 1925, was as follows: Shoes hurt her terribly and she took them to shoemaker to be fixed. He slit or prepared something to put in them, when that something seemed to explode and turn into two American flags high up in the air, which she and shoemaker tried to reach, but the flags were too high up. The shoemaker finally got the shoes fixed such that they were comfortable on her feet, when she looked down to note that her fine silk stockings were full of holes. You will give the interpretations of these dreams and the lessons to be gained from same.

EC: Yes, we have the body here, and the dreams with their lessons as may be gained from these. In giving this we must first take into consideration the conditions surrounding the mental forces of the body through which these dreams or visions were given. While the body does have the dreams and the relations as are found between the conscious existence of forces in self and that as reached through the subconscious forces of the body, there have been few that the body retains in their entirety, yet portions of same often are brought to the consciousness of the individual.

Then, we find the individual, [106], under the present stress of conditions, physically and mentally, brings these, as it were, to the consciousness of self through these existent conditions. And these as we find are emblematical of conditions existent in those surrounding the individual and pertaining to the foundation, as in shoes, for the individual and for those about the body.

The seeking to have someone assist in preparing the foundation is that represented in going to someone to seek assistance. With the sudden explosion is indicated the change entirely that is to occur from the manner in which the foundations are to be prepared or made.

The flying away of flag is emblematical of the heights of two different ways, yet made the same, as both are of the same nature in flag.

The inability to reach same by self, and the help sought, indicates the manner that each shall go above that necessary of help from either.

With the preparation of the foundation for use, and the finding of the rents in the apparel, is shown the faulty conditions the entity may obtain in self through the manner of seeking the aid.

The lessons then are apparent in the explanation of what this means.

Reading 39-3

MHB: Now you will have before you the body of [39], present in this room, and the enquiring mind of this body, who had the dream I will give you during the course of the past six years. At various times during the past six years the body has experienced the following: Visualized airship heavier than air, which collects its lifting and driving force from the atmosphere by means of points on the top of it. Underneath this machine there are apparently two heavy copper bars running the length of it, having small points underneath, which when charged with the force lifts the machine from the air apparently neutralizing the force of gravity. The machine was driven by the power streaming from points attached to the rear. You will give the interpretation of this dream or vision, tell us if such a machine is practical and if such a power is available, and how such may be made. You will answer questions regarding this.

EC: Yes, we have the body, the enquiring mind, [39], here. With dreams and visions as come to individual, these are of various classes and groups, and are the emanations from the conscious, subconscious, or superconscious, or the combination and correlation of each, depending upon the individual and the personal development of the individual, and are to be used in the lives of such for the betterment of such individual.

In this vision, we find this emblematical condition being presented to the entity. Not wholly a condition that may not be made feasible, plausible, workable, or used in the operation of man's endeavor; yet to the entity is as an emblematical condition, with those of the conscious forces using that which the mind has dwelt upon to show the higher forces as are to be used by the entity in the spiritual, mental, and physical development for same and as we see in the various presentations of the vision, the slight changes that occur in the make-up of the machine show the various amount of endeavor within the mental forces of the entity to gain the understanding of same; for, as is seen, there will appear this same vision three other periods in the development of the entity, and in each there will be seen again changes as are to come in the entity's understanding of the emanations, or the abilities of individuals to apply in the life of an entity in material plane the various lessons as are attained or gained from same. As is seen, all of the power must come from above. The bars representing, then, as the individual's foundation, upon which there is given the lifting power of same to soar through the various fields of knowledge in attaining the various points necessary for that development and that understanding to apply such forces in the material plane. Just as is seen in the various points from the machine, shows that all force, while as of one, is gained through the various sources and contacts as are made, and is called in the material plane that of the environmental forces, while in that of the hereditary forces is as that left in the wake of the impelling force that drives the body and the mind through those spaces necessary to make the individual one in all of its applications in the various fields of endeavor, whether studying the higher fields of thought or in making the turns or curves in the various walks of life, and in the individuals as the entity contacts from time to time.

In the application of same as from the field of the purely mechanical forces, these—as they are presented from time to time—will bring to the knowledge of the individual that as is necessary to bring about the changes in mechanical appliance of that force known as the earth–side force as has been applied in eons ago to those crafts that soared through the ether. [See Life reading 39-2.]

Be satisfied with that attained from the experience, until there is through a little here, a little there, line upon line, precept upon precept—applying that already gained, that more may be given unto thee.

Ready for questions.

(Q) The entity, then, may seek this source for further information on coming experiences?

(A) The entity may seek all sources—for, as is seen, there are many points toward the heavens, as of the lifting power. The stability of self—as is set in those bars that lift or parallel with the earth—must be kept in that brightness as is seen, that there may be attained more power, more force, in the applying in self that already attained.

(Q) That is all of the questions in this reading.

(A) We are through with this reading for the present for much may be given to the entity as respecting its (the entity's) development, mentally, spiritually, physically.

Use that in hand—or the simple rod stretched over the mighty sea became the power in the hands of him who walked with the Creative Energy—God. The withered rod became the budded almond in the hands of him who sought to know His ways, and applied same in the life. Keep thine paths straight. Walk in the shadow of His wing. Keep thine eyes, thine heart, ever to that source from which emanates all power that lifts man toward the Creator.

Reading 137-36

(Q) Night of November 25, or morning of November 26. A headless man in uniform of a sailor was walking in an erect manner with either a gun or a cane in his hand.

(A) Seeing things. This, as we see, the developing of those forces in the entity wherein the physical projection of spiritual elements come to the entity in certain stages of the condition of the body, physically, mentally, see? And as this is seen, one in arms or one in uniform, or one in the action of defense or in duty, see—this, then, to the entity the lesson: Do not lose the head too much in duty as seen, to accomplish the greater lessons as may be learned from the association of ideas as pertain to things more spiritual.

(Q) *A man approached many, including myself, in what seemed to be a hotel lobby. When he first approached us he had the appearance of a detective, but as he drew near I had the feeling that he was Jesus Christ.*

(A) In this there is seen, in the correlation of these conditions as passing through that in groups, in the individual, in the mass even, there, in the form of man, as man to man, may come to the entity these spirit forces as would guide and mean as much to the individual as the life, as the living, as the example, of the Christ's coming means to the whole world; these forces as come in man may mean as much to this entity, when applied spiritually.

(Q) *There was something I felt related to the vision I previously had had regarding an arrow shot from a bow, and which a reading interpreted was an indication of a message to come to me of powerful intent and purpose, but just what that something was in this particular vision I cannot now remember. Recall the vision to me, interpret and give me the lesson.*

(A) As is seen first in the vision of the arrow shot into the air, going high and strong, and as the interpretation, the lesson, was that to the entity there would be presented those visions, or those truths coming as the greatest truth, or greatest purpose in the life, these as we see here are presented in these two as seen, headless soldier with cane or defense weapon, the Master walking into the group.

Reading 136–41

(Q) *Saturday or Sunday night, July 17 or 18, 1926. [900] and I were on a boat and there seemed much thundering or shooting and fighting. It ended with the boat being struck by lightening and the boiler exploding. It sank. We were blown up—killed.*

(A) Now in this, while there will be those conditions that will remind the entity, somewhat, of this vision, the real lesson we find being those of the emblematical conditions. Boat—the voyage of life. Trip, or the passage on same—the change that will come in the affairs of the entity. And the relations with each, and the conditions following, being those of some turmoil, some troubles. Yet in the blowing up representing the change, or the settling down to the more perfect understanding in each, see?

Then, let this condition be as the warning for both, that the paths of each be made more in accord one with the other, see?

Reading 136–45

(Q) *Morning of September 5. Mother . . . and her home in Indiana. There seemed to be ghosts there.*

(A) Rather that indication of those fears, those thoughts that do enter in regarding the physical health of individuals of this household. Ghosts, then, of the mind, see? fear.

Reading 341–15

(Q) *Night of 26, or morning of 27, October, 1925. Dreamed of being picked up by an elephant. May have been more—Recall—*

(A) As this is seen, the elephant as represents power, might, cunning, with all the mental proclivities of that gained through knowledge. Then let the entity be picked up by same, studying to show the abilities to use and apply same in the manner as acceptable unto Him, as is seen in the rescue from the elephant by the keeper, see?

Reading 136–18

(Q) *Tuesday morning, November 3, 1925. Ma, [900] and I were living together in a house at New Jersey, and I heard much shooting and excitement. All of the windows of our house were open, and as it was raining and storming out, we rushed to close and lock them. Some terrible wild man seemed to be running through the town shooting and causing great trouble, and the police were chasing him.*

(A) (breaking in) The large man, the bugaboo, that comes to the entity in these emblematical conditions here presented, and as seen in others, is in self and self's temper, see?

(Q) *(Continuing) Conditions were chaotic and troublesome. We stopped the police to ask if they had caught this terrible person and they answered, "Not yet."*

(A) Then the answer we would see: Control self, if this terrible person would be caught and conquered, see?

Reading 136–6

(Q) *Dreamed I died.*

(A) This is the manifestation of the birth of thought and mental development awakening in the individual, as mental forces and physical forces develop. This, then, is the awakening of the subconscious, as is manifested in death in physical forces, being the birth in the mental.

Reading 341–13

(Q) *Dreamed of being at . . . , Kentucky, at home. Two people seemed to be with me. We were watching a dirigible and an airship that were sailing above us but seemed to be in great distress. Suddenly the dirigible spun on its nose and crashed into the ground in the lawn. I heard the cries and groans of the occupants as the ship struck. The two other people and I started towards the wreck but were at first warned back by those who survived. A little later we were called on to help carry the injured ones to the house. The man I carried seemed to have hurt his leg and kept crying not to take his leg off. Later it seemed that I was again at the wreck. I drank something from a bottle and then continued to collect tools, a hammer and other things.*

(A) In this, again the emblematical conditions of life presented to the entity.

In that of the dirigible and flying machine, those high ideals as are held in the entity's mind, without stability, showing the destructive forces as may come to such without that strength of character in the tried and true ways to be stable, and the assistance as is seen is the call of self to aid self, as it were, in that way the entity would take.

The assistance and the call not to take or remove portion of body, rather that the entity sees in the self conditions that may arise, making this such necessary in the life's work, see? to remove portions of same, unless kept in that straight and narrow way.

The taking from the bottle, rather that necessary, for this represents, then, the water or the assistance of life, presented in that straight and narrow way.

The gathering, then, of tools, that necessary working paraphernalia for the successes the entity would accomplish. The lesson, then, is seen.

Reading 2671–5

(Q) *Morning of May 6, 1927. I was standing in the back yard of my home—had my coat on. I felt something inside the cloth on the cuff of my left hand coat sleeve. I worked it out, but it was fastened in the cloth and broke off as it came out, leaving part in. It proved to be a cocoon and where broke a small black spider came out. The cocoon was black and left a great number of eggs—small ones—on my coat sleeve, which I began to break and pull off. The spider grew fast and ran away, speaking plain English as it ran, but that I do not remember, except that it was saying something about its mother. The next time I saw it, it was a large black spider which I seemed to know was the same one grown up, almost as large as my fist—had a red spot on it, otherwise was a deep black. At this time it had gotten into my house and had built a web all the way across the back inside the house and was comfortably watching me. I took a broom, knocked it down and out of the house, thinking I'd killed it, but it did more talking at that time. I remember putting my foot on it and thought it was dead. The next time I saw it, it had built a long web from the ground on the outside of the house in the back yard, near where I first got it out of my sleeve—and it was running up toward the eaves fast when it saw me. I couldn't reach it but threw my straw hat in front of it and cut the web and spider fell to the ground, talking again, and that time I hacked it to pieces with my knife.*

(A) In this there is seen the emblematical conditions of those forces as are being enacted in the life of this body. And, as is seen, both the spider and the character of same are as warnings to the body as respecting the needs of the body taking a definite stand as respecting the relations of others who would in this underhand manner take away from the body those surroundings of the home—that are in the manner of being taken, unless such a stand is taken. For, as is seen, the conditions of the relations of the entity, the body, with another, as seen, are of the nature as is emblematically shown by the relations of this body with this other body; that its relations at first meant only that of the casual conditions that might be turned to an account of good, in a social and financial manner; yet, as has been seen, there has come the constant drain on the entity, not only in pocket but in the affections of the heart, and now such threaten the very foundations of the home—and, as seen, threaten to separate the body from the home and its surroundings; and unless the entity attacks this condition, cutting same out of the mind, the body, the relations, the conditions, there will come that condition that will be, as it were, as the condition as seen.

Take the warning then. Prepare self. Meet the conditions as the man, not as the weakling—and remember those duties that the body owes first to those to whom the sacred vows were given, and to whom the entity and body owes its position in every sense, and as well as the duty that is obligatory to the body or those to whom the entity, the body, should act in the sense of the defender, rather than bringing through such relations those dark underhanded sayings, as are seen, as said by that one who would undermine, as well as are being said by those whom the body may feel such relations are hidden from; yet these have grown to such extent as may present a menace to the very heart and soul of the *body* of this entity. Beware! Beware!

Editor's Note: [2671-5]'s wife wrote Edgar Cayce to say that her husband was having an affair.

Reading 140–10

(Q) *Night of Tuesday, December 15, or Wednesday morning, December 16, 1925. We were in the country—on a party it seemed at Rose Fenton Farm, Asbury Park, New Jersey. We started to drive away from this restaurant over a lakeside road. Everyone was getting into their motor cars preparatory to the homeward drive. I had a two seater, new green Pierce Arrow Car. [137] climbed in next to me—I was driving, and as we started down the lakeside road, we kept close to the embankment and all at once I seemed to go over the edge. The car stopped and I thought to myself I could jam on the emergency brake and have it hold long enough for us all to get out and escape injury, but instead I did nothing. I jumped out of the car and into the lake, the car falling after me and on top of me. I was killed.*

(A) In this there is presented to the entity the phenomena, in this emblematical manner, pertaining to that condition in the mental forces, which pertains to the condition in life. That is, that the time for preparation for any condition is when there is the time, or before a condition appears in which the energies, the abilities, the conditions of all force are presented for the entity to exercise therein, see? for, as is seen, the life is filled with the beauties in life, the enjoyment of the pleasures of the flesh in every manner; yet when the emergency presents itself, although the action of the mind is to *do*, without the trained responding of the physical to that action, there is the loss. That is, then: To know to do good and do it not, to him it is imputed as sin. This lesson is manifested to the entity here. Use it. No special significance as to a given time, place or condition, but as relates to Life, see?

Reading 137–31

(Q) *Wednesday evening, November 11, 1925. Someone (probably myself) was looking up to corner of a tent of some kind and the person (probably me) seemed to be ordering God.*

(A) As is seen in this emblematical form, the entity gains through this the understanding wherein the spiritual forces in the physical being may so magnify self's interests as to come under that direct influence of those spiritual laws. And as the tents represent to the entity the insecure dwelling, and the looking up and ordering to the High and Holy, that which the entity, through the prayer of the righteous many may be saved, and as the ordering is then to self, to so direct life in self as to be in that closer accord, closer touch, that the orders from the Highest may be through that channel from which entity has seen much development, see? Well that in this connection entity read Jude, especially 10th, 11th and 12th verses.

Reading 136–26

(Q) *Monday morning, December 28, 1925. I saw handwriting on the wall, with "Well." I didn't understand and went back to sleep and saw myself in a blue and white dress. I was kneeling down on my knees before the doctor and he patted me on the head and I said: "Through you and God Almighty has our mother been spared to us," and then he said, "Let us pray again to you and the Lord God."*

(A) In this there is presented to the entity that, as has been given, under the conditions there is only then for the entity to put self into the hands of the giver of all good and perfect gifts. For in choosing the physician, the best, then for self and for the good of the condition that is presented. The blue and white giving then the pure, the true self in that prayer and supplication, and with this perfect understanding there comes the "All is well," see? for as the handwriting is of old, this then comes to this body, that the full understanding of the abilities of self are so limited, and only in Him would we put our trust if all would be well with ourselves.

Reading 136-24

(Q) Dreaming, said out loud, "[900], don't eat so many coats."

(A) As this presents an unreasonable condition in that as said, it presents an unreasonable attitude of the individual towards [900] in some respect. Then be in that manner not unreasonable, see?

Reading 195-42

(Q) Early hours of Sunday morning, July 3, 1927, at . . . , Ohio. Dreamed that I was going to some kind of a meeting at night. I was walking through hilly country taking high road. Noticed someone walking on lower road. I crossed over ruins of old home, recognizing the old home of my uncle (Geo. S. [. . .] of San Gabriel, California), which is near new home. Thought how nice it would be to see all the family after the meeting. Crossed an old fountain—there was an obstruction around fountain. I climbed the fence—was accosted by young military guards, seemingly boy scouts— was escorted before some tribunal and asked to give account of myself. I said I was from . . . , Ohio, formerly from California. Gave full details. I was told my case was under consideration and I left. Seemed to be on a boat overlooking much water when one of the guards said I was wanted. I followed, and tribunal said after considering my case I was to be court-martialed next day—that I should give matter thought and could either defend myself or have someone defend me. I left soon and the thought came to me to have my cousin Major Geo. S. [. . .] defend me.

(A) In this we find there are seen the emblematical conditions as respecting meeting contemplated by the entity, and the entering in an association with same. As is seen when the entity climbs to that source from which—as represented by the fount, or that place from which the greater knowledge may be obtained—there is seen the line of the criticism as may be expected by the entity from so doing; yet, as is seen, there is then opened—by this gaining a portion of knowledge—the greater expanse of knowledge than even from the fount, in the large amount of water as is seen associated when the entity is called to the tribunal. The thought, the intent, the purport in self to have *officer* address or defend the entity, is as from those sources upon which the entity may call for the better understanding of all of life. And as each applies in the life the entity may gain through same that knowledge wherein the greater development comes to the entity, irrespective of censure or of any criticism that may be presented by others. For, as is seen, the presentation of criticism is as of the raw recruit, or of ones of little understanding. Be not afraid. Rather gain that claim whereupon the greater understanding, and the ability to apply same, may come into the life of self.

Reading 137–99

EC: We have the body, the enquiring mind, [137]—this we have had here before.

The dreams, as we see, to this body bring much of those elements that are as the weighing of matters, conditions, elements, in the mental mind with the subconscious forces and experiences of the body, and come in emblematical or in direct response to desire of the mental body to acquaint self with the more perfect understanding. Hence, as has oft been given, the body is nearer to that point where the mystic or the subconscious self may be applied than most individuals, for much has been experienced through the physical planes by the entity—much may be expected, then, of the applications to which the entity lends self in its endeavors.

(Q) *Of recent date. I was sitting at my desk in the office in an argument with [my husband] [900]. It seemed we were going to separate, and he said he was going to do something to me. I said, "you've got a swell chance."*

(A) This in this direct manner relates to those conditions, as has oft been given, that these are as helpmeets one to another, and that without the strength and the encouragement from the other, *neither* would accomplish that as may be done in unison; for the changes in the life of each is that the activity of one is that necessary balance for the better understanding of the other.

Then, as the warning—let not that in any manner enter the life that would separate the self from the abilities of the other, for in this union of strength much may be attained by each. Let the minds of each, then, depend mentally, morally, physically, upon the works and activities of the other, mentally, morally, physically.

Reading 900–114

(Q) *Then my mother, wife and I, took an automobile ride, and I observed all the things that money could buy, and also observed the glory of the True Life. I saw trains and boats and also the entrance to what seemed a monastery. I said to my mother: "What is the use of making money and those things the object of life, when they aren't even real?"*

(A) This again, we see, viewing the same perspective vision from a different angle, gaining then, as it were, in this that perspective of the valuation of the real and unreal, for as has been given, and well summed in this: "Though a man gain the *whole world* and lose his own soul" of what use is it? and as is viewed, these, as precepts and principles, must become the workableness of the entity, for as is seen, with the closer associations of the mental forces to those of the truths as pertain to the phenomena of life, these insights in same are gained, making a clearer vision, a clearer understanding the full meaning, and in same we become free indeed. Not then that each in its sphere is to be belittled but that each is made to serve its intent and purpose, to magnify even as He would magnify.

Reading 2205-3

(Q) Explain the significance of the childhood dream of eyes and bubbles, and how its influence can be used for good in the future.

(A) These as we find are, as it were, the ends—or portions—of many individual experiences of the entity through many of its sojourns. As the entity knew of and saw manifestations of the power of the unseen forces in the experiences of others, it brought those activities and movements of every form. Thus these become as fearful experiences, or as things that create fear. Yet if they are taken as assurances of His promises, it will be seen that they are reminders that out of self visions come, out of self thoughts arise, out of self activities may begin; and these become rather then as stepping-stones than stumbling stones—as they oft have.

Then, the little assurances that arise, bless them, keep them; not as fearful things, but as those things upon which *hope* and faith and patience and love may be builded!

Editor's Note: Dream guidance on specific issues.

Reading 137–60

(Q) Arthur De Cordova asked me if [5768] was away, to which I replied in affirmative. He then said: "Well, then you are going to make some money." I jumped to the conclusion he meant Fleischman but he corrected me by telling me that Ajax Rubber stock ought to go up because of the commodity Rubber going up. Also some reference in this respect to Fisk Tire bonds. De Cordova and I looked at the Ajax specialist book (which I have on the floor) but I was not favorable to buying any Ajax rubber stock, so we did nothing.

(A) Then, as seen, this the continuation of that as given, that the entity, physically, should study these conditions, in the physical, mental, way and manner as pertains to these individual stocks, see? that the use of such conditions, as would be determined by the study of same, may be used by the entity.

(Q) What is indicated I should do in regard to Ajax Rubber? When?

(A) Study, study, study, study! Not any indication of buying, or selling either.

Reading 853–5

(Q) How may I develop my dreams and visions so as to enable me to locate the hidden treasure?

(A) By not wishing or not insisting, but as of preparation of self; meditations and then turning—as it were—to the within that there may be the visions of those activities that will aid not only those that would assist from beyond but aid self in recalling and seeing the places and positions of the cache.

Reading 853–8

(Q) How may I best prepare self for meditation and then turn within, as previously given, to locate buried treasure to aid those that would assist from beyond and aid me in recalling and seeing places and positions of cache?

(A) Study first those associations of what the mental mind is, and how the mental mind (that is, the mind of the body) may be attuned with the Infinite or to the soul mind. For they are—as Life—one and the same; not as sections, but as an awareness, as a remembrance, as an activity.

And entering into meditation (as we have given in the pamphlet on Meditation) one then submerges the physical consciousness and allows an attunement; as an acoustic instrument would be, as a recalling to mind would be; so that there is then opened for the self the remembrance.

As has been given for this entity, such an attunement or such an awareness becomes most in accord in dream; for then there is the submerging of the physical consciousness and the desires of same; and if there is the meditating it brings better attunement with less of what may be termed as an interference of conscious forces, conscious influences.

Hence, as has been given, if this will be practiced or applied in the experience, the remembrance should come.

Editor's Note: Recurring dreams.

Reading 487–6

GC: You will have before you the body and the enquiring mind of [487] of . . . , Virginia, this dream the body had three nights in succession, February 23, 24, 25, 1926, all regarding the same thing, three little wagons. You will give the interpretation and lesson to be gained from these.

EC: Now, we have this developing mind of an entity that becomes impressed with those visions as are presented to the consciousness, through the subconscious or subliminal self and these are presented that the entity, in the study and thought that may be put on same, for the entity's good and edification. That is, that the entity may better understand self, and self's application to conditions as arise in its life.

As is seen, the wagons as seen present that as an intent or desire, or purpose in the life. Something desired to be done, something desired to be accomplished, something to be desired to give the correct impression to individuals. As is seen in how that the wagons are used, and all are presented—three in each time, see?—the three conditions as are presented in self. These, as they are given, and as they are used, are as but the way and manner in which self may train, govern, guard, direct self for the better control of self, as the wagons in their shape, their position, need the control. First, as is seen, a long desire—long wagon. As is seen, it is to and from those closely associated with the self, and is as how self would desire to treat, to be held in esteem by those individuals. As is seen in the next, the new white, red and striped wagon. Again, as is seen, associated with members of individual family. Then, representing truth, purity, and untruth, and as is seen in the red wagon that brings trouble, that brings the misunderstandings, then, as the entity sees, mis-understandings bring trouble to self, care to others, worry to many. As is again seen in wagons of peculiar type or construction, and as associ-ated with other individuals rather than of the family, again in the study of same is seen how that the temperament, the attitude, the disposition, makes for good and bad influences. Then, those responsible for the individuality of the entity, and for the development of its purposes in life, should apply same in the way and manner to the life of entity that he may gain good from same.

Reading 823–1

(Q) *Why in early childhood did I dream so many times that the world was being destroyed, always seeing a black destructive cloud?*

(A) From the experience in the Atlantean land, when there were those destructive forces as indicated. The entity saw or lived through those experiences of at least two, yea three, of the destructive periods; saw the land breaking up, as it were.

Editor's Note: Note Cayce's repeated emphasis on the importance of application.

Reading 294–70

Dreams, visions, impressions, to the entity in the normal sleeping state are the presentations of the experiences necessary for the devel-opment, if the entity would apply them in the physical life. These may be taken as warnings, as advice, as conditions to be met, conditions to be viewed in a way and manner as lessons, as truths, as they are pre-sented in the various ways and manners.

Reading 136–62

EC: Yes, we have the body, the enquiring mind, [136]. This we have had here before. The dreams again and again present to the entity those lessons, those truths, that the entity seeks to apply in the life, and as these are presented may the entity take those warnings and those lessons from same, and applying same in the life brings about those things that bring more peace, more satisfaction, and a better understanding of the conditions, the purposes, and all of life—for it is not all of life to live, nor yet all of death to die.

Reading 903-5

Apply those applications as have been seen. More of these may come to thee, would thou apply same. If thou desirest thou may *have* more of these direct. If thou fearest, do not call.

Reading 136-45

The dreams, the visions, the impressions as are gained in experiences through the subconscious forces, are giving to the entity those lessons, as may be applied in the physical body, the physical mind, and in the material manner, as has been outlined for the body. The lessons as are being gained by same are as the truths that come by the entity making itself in an attunement and an at-onement with those universal forces, into which the body-conscious mind enters when in the somnambulistic state, or in sleep: for the subconscious force operates on.

Use same, then, and apply same for the better conditions, the better understanding of life and life's purposes, and of those conditions through which the entity passes. For each experience *applied* is a development for the entity. Without an application of the experience is to act in that way that brings condemnation, or a mis-application of the advantages as may be gained by knowledge.

Editor's Note: John Van Auken, in an essay titled "River of Dreams," offers this counsel on working with dreams:

> It is important to recognize that the dreamer is our inner self. Therefore, the best interpreter is our inner self, so we should obtain the interpretation while still in or near the dreaming self. Trying to translate a dream later with only

our outer, three-dimensional self is very difficult. It did not dream the dream. We will do much better if we keep the body and outer self still as we awaken, and get the dream and its meaning from the inner self.

Here are some quick steps toward better interpretation:

1. Watch your mood upon waking. This will give you the best sense of whether the inner self is happy or unhappy about conditions.

2. Get the gist of the dream first, details second. Jesus once observed that we tend to strain for gnats while we are swallowing camels. The big picture, the overriding theme, is much more important for us to grasp than the details.

3. Understand that the subconscious may use exaggeration to get our attention. It's like the joke of how to get your mule to do something: first, you hit him as hard as you can to get his attention. In a similar manner the subconscious gets our attention: exaggerated activities and shocking imagery will do more to get our attention than sweetly whispered instructions. Therefore, don't let the dramatic exaggerations overwhelm you or cause fear. In fact, the bizarre image or activity is likely the key to interpreting the entire dream.

4. Dreams are usually symbolic. They speak in imagery that represents more than literal appearance. Like good parables or novelettes, they tell a story that has a deeper meaning than the details. Often they use figures of speech. For example, if I told you that I really put my foot in my mouth while talking with someone yesterday, you would know that I did not literally put my foot in my mouth. Dreams speak in the same manner and are best interpreted as you would figures of speech.

5. Finally, nothing will help us get better dream guidance than using dream content in our lives. Create an action plan for each dream. Ask yourself, How can I use this dream in my life today? Even if you are not really sure of the dream's meaning, attempt to use some portion of it. In this way your inner self will be stimulated to bring more insight and guidance through the dream channel, and it will become clearer and more relevant.

In the Book of Job it is written: "God speaks once, even twice—though man regards it not—in a dream, in a vision of the night, when deep sleep falls upon man, in slumberings upon the bed. Then God opens the ears of humans, and seals their instruction, that He may withdraw man from his [selfish] purposes, and hide pride from man. He keeps back his soul from the pit, and his life from perishing by the sword."

Budget time for swimming in the river of dreams. They guide us to the shores of paradise. Sleep is a shadow of death and the life beyond this world. To live in dreamy sleep is to know heaven.

3

●

Dreams and ESP

Reading 136–54

(Q) *Morning of December 27, 1926. Dreamed Emmie committed suicide.*

(A) This shows to the entity, through this correlation of mental forces of the body–mind itself and those of the body–mind of Emmie, that such conditions had passed through this mind—contemplation of such conditions, see? They have passed.

(Q) *Is Emmie contemplating any such act as suicide? Will she carry it out?*

(A) They have passed.

(Q) *How did [136] get this information about Emmie in dream?*

(A) Correlation of subconscious minds that contact through thought, for thoughts are deeds and may become crimes or miracles. Just as given in the introduction, as it were, here dreams are the correlation of various phases of the mentality of the individual, see? and individual meaning of that entity. Dreams are those of conditions wherein there may be taken into the body–physical that of elements that produce hallucinations, or the activity of that induced in the system in itself attempting to take on its individual force produces hallucinations, nightmares, or abortions to the mental forces of an individual. See how the connection becomes then between the individual mind and that producing same? The same as we find, there may be conditions from the mental mind of an entity, by deep study or thought, wherein the experiences of the individual entity are correlated through the subconscious forces of the entity—the latent forces of the entity—the hidden forces of the entity—and correlating same in a vision or dream. Often these are as symbolic conditions, each representing a various phase to the mental development of the entity.

Others there are, a correlation between mentalities or subconscious entities, wherein there has been attained, physically or mentally, a correlation of individual ideas or mental expressions that bring from one subconscious to another those of actual existent conditions, either direct or indirect, to be acted upon or that are ever present, see?

Hence we find visions of the past, visions of the present, visions of the future. For to the subconscious there is no past or future—all present. This would be well to remember in much of the information as may be given through such forces as these.

Reading 137–17

Editor's Note: This reading was given for a stockbroker who was using dreams for investment information

(Q) July 12, or early Monday morning, July 13, 1925. Dreamed a man was trying to sell me a radio. Then someone put poison on the doorknob of my door and urged me to come and touch it. I was terribly frightened. He tried to force me to touch the poisoned knob. Struggling, I awakened in a cold sweat.

(A) In this we have a presentation to this mind of conditions that are to arise in the physical affairs of the body. The presentation of a sale attempting to be made of radio refers to the deal that will be offered the individual in radio stocks or corporations, or such natures, offering as a wonderful proposition to the body. The presentation of poison being placed by someone on the door represents the condition that would enter into same, if the body were to accept or to invest in such conditions, corporations or stocks, of that nature. Hence the warning as would come from this at the present, or during this time—next sixteen to twenty days: Do not invest in stocks, bonds, or any conditions pertaining to radio activity work.

Reading 136–7

(Q) June 27, at home. Dreamed of an automobile accident.

(A) Again the projection of conditions as were discussed in the conscious physical mind, with the projection from consciousness to subconscious conditions and presented in an accident that happened to other individuals, seen but not experienced by the individuals themselves. No lesson, other than that the mind, dwelling upon physical conditions, partakes in the subconscious condition those of like element; showing then how definitely what one thinks in reality in inner self one becomes or partakes of.

(Q) Monday, June 29. Dreamed of a weak-minded boy or child.

(A) Again the projection of thoughts, conditions, as expressed in physical manner, and showing how again that projections come from the conscious to subconscious forces and visions seen of one in such states. This, then, is again how the conscious forces feed the subconscious, and for the better indwelling of the subconscious, good and *only* good thoughts should be projected into the subconscious, for developments come through such; for the body (internally speaking) becomes that upon which it feeds. Hence, true has it been said, "When I was a child I thought as a child. Now I become a man I put away childish thoughts." In like manner ones developing, when they carry those thoughts in conversation, or in the deeper recesses of mind concerning conditions, we see projections of same in the subconscious reaction through dreams; for dreams are that of which the subconscious is made, for any conditions ever becoming reality is first dreamed. [Her son, [142], was a mental case 25 years later.]

Reading 137–118

(Q) Will my wife precede me in death and will I be able to foretell my own death as given in the prophecy?

(A) Even as thine earthly brother gave, "I go up to be bound of those that know not what they do"—even so will self be able to know within self that which is to take place in material planes. Be not overcome by much knowledge. Be not overdone nor undone by that as may be given. Remember, mine son, that thou saidst of him who *did* wage war—even with Him—concerning the body of Moses, whom thou may even direct—that though he recognized his power, yet railed he not—but said, "God will deal with thee." Not of thine *own* power may these forces be done—but flesh and blood may manifest a spiritual truth, but may not *order* a spirit in *any* direction! Aid and succor may come *through* flesh and blood, even to those near the pit—yet there is fixed that impassable gulf, and he that makes his will one *with* the *father* may be committed a care through His direction. Keep that as is given, my son, and err not in well-doing; for oft, as has been said, those that call upon the forces only in distress may be heard from afar. Keep thine self *close*, that those that would direct may be ever near thee—for the stumbling block *always* lies in self-aggrandizement of power and ability stored in one's own self, in the misuse of self in relation one to another. Keep the faith, My Son Keep the faith—

Reading 294–131

Editor's Note: According to Harmon Bro, "Cayce, when awake, wondered about the outreach that occurred in his readings and in his dreams. Accordingly, he dreamed about his question. This dream, like a number he had, occurred while he was in trance, talking and concentrating on someone's need. A part of his mind was still available for a dream, even during a reading. Shortly after the loss of his hospital, when he was questioning the value of his gift after all, he received the following reading regarding a dream:"

EC: Yes, we have the body, the enquiring mind, [294], present in this room—this we have had before. The dreams or visions, or both, as they are presented, represent either some development or warning, that there may be the better understanding of the various conditions and the activities that are active with the efforts of the body, in the attempt to bring to others that concept which will make for developments of individuals along the varied lines of expressions of the individuals, or the body itself. Ready for dreams.

(Q) [GC read dream had Jan. 15, 1932 during reading 3985-1]: *Saw myself fixing to give a reading, and the process through which a reading was gotten. Someone described it to me. There was a center or spot from which, on going into the state, I would radiate upward. It began as a spiral, except there were rings all around—*

commencing very small, and as they went on up they got bigger and bigger. The spaces in between the rings were the various places of development which individuals had attained, from which I would attempt to gain information. That was why a very low developed body might be so low that no one even giving information would be able to give anything that would be worthwhile. There were certain portions of the country that produced their own radiation; for instance, it would be very much easier to give a reading for an individual who was in the radiation that had to do with health, or healing; not necessarily in a hospital, but in a healing radiation—than it would be for an individual who was in purely a commercial radiation. I might be able to give a much better reading (as the illustration was made) for a person in Rochester, N.Y., than one in Chicago, Ill., because the vibrations of Rochester were very much higher than the vibrations in Chicago. The closer the individual was to one of the rings, the easier it would be to get the information. An individual would, from any point in between, by their own desire go toward the ring. If just curious, they would naturally draw down towards the center away from the ring, or in the spaces between the rings. [See also 1/33 EC's repeated dream, since mid 20's of being tiny dot seeking light, under 294-19 Reports.]

(A) This vision is recognizable as an experience of the soul, or the *entity*, in activity. There have been various formulas or descriptions of how information for a body was obtained through these channels. There has been promised, through these channels, that there was to be a greater awakening to this entity in its field of endeavor. So in this way there is, as indicated, a way of the information being better correlated, better understood by individuals–who are through that as may be termed the attunements of the various directions, in the various portions of the country or world–of their relationship to the actual fact of seeking through the channels. [See 262-16.] As indicated, the entity is—in the affairs of the world—a tiny speck, as it were, a mere grain of sand; yet when raised in the atmosphere or realm of the spiritual forces it becomes all inclusive, as is seen by the size of the funnel—which reaches not downward, nor outward, nor over, but direct to that which is felt by the experience of man as into the heavens itself. As indicated in the rings, or the nets as of nerves, each portion of the sphere, or the earth, or the heavens, is in that place which has been set by an All Wise Creative Energy. Each may attain to those relationships by that which is attempted in the activities of an individual, a group, a class, a mass, a nation. In that manner do they create their position in the affairs of the universe. Each speck, as an atom of human experience, is connected one with another as the continuity of the cone seen, and in the manner that the nerves of an animating or living object bears upon that in its specific center, but reaches to the utmost portions of the universality of force or activity in the whole universe, and has its radial effect upon one another.

As the entity, then, raises itself through those activities of subjugating or making as null those physical activities of the body, using only—as it were (in the cone)—the trumpet of the universe, in reaching out for that being sought, each entity—or each dot, then—in its respective sphere—acts as the note or the lute in action, that *voices* that which may come forth from such seeking.

Then we find, in the classification, in the activity of those that correlate such information, those in the various spheres will naturally classify themselves—even as given in the illustration, that there will more often be the sound of help to those in Rochester than to those in Chicago. That only as an illustration. Not that there may not be as much healing to those from the one as the other, but the effect upon the individual in the environ makes for the tone which resounds from that received. See? This should, then, be a helpful illustration to those correlating in understanding and classifying the information that may be received. This should, to the body giving information, make known to him that there is being *opened* an access to the Thrones themselves! See? [See 262-16; 1/33 See 294-131, Par. R3, HLC's paper, How Edgar Cayce Gives a Psychic Reading, using above 2-Q & 2-A.]

Reading 900-248

Editor's Note: It's fascinating to note that Cayce corroborated a similar explanation for outreach outlined in an unforgettable dream experience reported by one of his trained dreamers. The reading refers to a hand drawn diagram submitted by Mr. [900], along with his questions.

(Q) July 1st, 2nd or 3rd. I was on a boat and entering a room, saw Mrs. [139] on the operating table. The man in white hospital garb who let me in, pointed to the doctor half sarcastically, half despairingly. "All he has done since she came in is to operate," he said. I went over and looked at her. There she lay, thin, wrinkled, para-

lyzed and unconscious. I picked her up and carried her out. She spoke to me and it seemed like the time she spoke to me before being taken to the hospital when she told me not to let them operate, as if they did so, she would not be with us anymore. So she spoke to me again, telling me she was dying. I tried, in a superfluous fashion, to encourage her and as I kissed her she said, or I experienced the feeling that she said: "This is the last time you will see me." Hopelessly I returned her to the operating table, where the doctor stood ready to operate, and I seemed to take a train. Our paths divided in opposite directions. . . .

Now as regards this communication—first was it a definite communication between my consciousness in the physical and another consciousness in the spiritual?

(A) Correct. Just as given.

(Q) Might it be represented as follows, regarding the drawing:

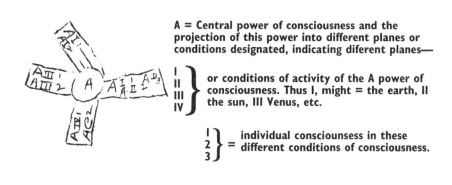

A = Central power of consciousness and the projection of this power into different planes or conditions designated, indicating diferent planes—

I
II
III
IV } **or conditions of activity of the A power of consciousness. Thus I, might = the earth, II the sun, III Venus, etc.**

1
2
3 } = **individual consciounsess in these different conditions of consciousness.**

(A) (Interrupting) phases of consciousness—better word.

(Q) (Continuing) all of which is in elemental substance; the A power of consciousness. I am then A I 1—an individual consciousness in physical form, yet embraced by the one A power, that may at this point, this common property that is part of all of us, (the subconscious), tune into any other individual consciousness that likewise takes its common source and property at point A, whether that other individual consciousness is part of plane II, III, or IV, etc. In other words, the road of my consciousness (memory we call the road) converges with every other road in the elements contained by the power of creation, but is different or individual only in embracing many awarenesses of these elements and my awareness and all the part development *that has led up to the present awareness may be made evident or is evident to every other developing awareness in so far as there is contained in my awareness that which is cognizable to another awareness. Thus I know the consciousness, [139], could fulfill her will to live or manifest further here on earth. I knew how this could be done and still know, and this other consciousness also felt I knew. Thus in my subconscious activity her awareness of this existent condition became one with my awareness and we became of one mind or One in that thought. Putting it differently, we became simply conscious companions of seeing one condition, and as our own awareness converges, as for example if you and I together think of the letter, K, we come into that contact with each other, or what we call thought communication and as the subconscious knows no space barriers, such communication may take place, (in the subconscious point A), between individual consciousness on any plane. Is this an explanation of spirit communication?*

(A) This is an explanation of spirit communication. As for the physical and the division of same from A, B, and from 1, 2, 3, these may be better designated as a circle, with the 5 points, as of a star, for this is rather that of the radiation from the one central force, that of the spirit force as is set in Him, the Creator and the Giver of all things, and as these are made one with that circle, from which the radiation of same would come, we would see these would diverge into the greater force, as we see, for, as has been given, "All heavens declare the glory of God," for in the higher realms of super-conscious, or the subconscious, an element of that superconscious, plus all radiated forces, or contacts through which the entity has passed to reach that present condition, whether advanced or debased, comes this one force that in *every* manifestation of the superconscious forces to the subconscious, or even to the lowest material-conscious, is that manifestation in those forms that would signify that consciousness from which same radiated, or as is seen in this: As this entity, [900], through that development of self, in making the will of the individual, or material-conscious, one with the subconscious, that communicates with the super-conscious or spiritual forces of the Universe, and their cosmic forces, position of recognizing the various conditions which may emanate or radiate through these various forms as are seen, and as each is brought into this consciousness of the entity, as to how these various forces may manifest, this then presents itself as a memory, as a thought, as an experience to the entity, in no uncertain manner, of not only the radiation of spirit force manifested in a material world, but of the good the entity may accomplish through things, would the entity bring self to that at-oneness, or to return to the first premise: Those that believe that God *is*, or would seek Him, should first believe He *is*—then act that way. That's the whole lesson.

4

●

Dreams, Visions, and Spiritual Growth

Editor's Note: Cayce often called "visions" the dreams that originate from the dreamer's higher self, the dreams that flow from the superconscious mind and the Universal Forces.

Reading 1904–2

Thus we find latent urges arising in visions, dreams, manifestations.

In thy reading (for ye are a greater interpreter of books, of writings of others), have ye not wondered why in the sacred writings it is said that God no longer spoke to man in visions or dreams? It is because man fed not his soul, his mind, upon things spiritual; thus closing the avenue or channel through which God might speak with the children of men.

Reading 958–3

For, He has not willed that any soul should perish. Thus it will behoove the entity to rely upon, and to search self deep, and to know that which is the prompting of the entity–as to whether the purpose and desire finds its inception in self-indulgences or in that which may enable others to take hope and to find that which brings harmony in their experience. . . .

Thus the injunction again to search deep within self, comparing motives, comparing desires, with that which is the entity's latent and manifested ideal.

Reading 262–9

(Q) [379]: Are my dreams ever significant of spiritual awakening?

(A) As is experienced by the entity, there are dreams and visions and experiences. When only dreams, these *too* are significant—but rather of that of the physical health, or physical conditions. In visions there is oft the *inter-between* giving expressions that make for an awakening between the mental consciousness, or that that has been turned over and over in the physical consciousness and mind being weighed with that the self holds as its ideal. In visions where spiritual awakenings, these most often are seen in symbols or signs, to the entity; for, as the training of self's consciousness in a manner of interpreting the visions would be in expressions of eye, hand, mouth, posture or the like, these are *interpreted* in thine own language. When these are, then, in symbols of such, know the awakening is at hand.

Reading 3175–1

[This is] one that has those abilities of vision, especially in dreams. These portend oft to happenings. These are well to consider; yet do not depend too much upon them, unless self is balanced well in its ideal and in its purpose.

Reading 2788–1

Keep thy humor. Keep the thinking well of self, but as well of thy neighbor.

Study to show thyself approved unto thy ideal. Learn and know what is thy ideal—spiritually, mentally, materially. Know in Whom ye have believed, as well as in what ye believe. Know the author of thy tenets, of thy faiths, of thy hopes, yea, of thy fears; studying to show thyself approved unto same, condemning none.

These, with the application of self in those directions indicated, will bring the entity to that place wherein it may be said of thee, "Well done; enter thou into the joys of thy Lord."

Reading 5754–2

Editor's Note: Because it bears so strongly on the topic of spiritual

dreams and vision, this section of Reading 5754-2 is repeated from an earlier chapter.

Hence we may find that an individual may from sorrow *sleep* and wake with a feeling of elation. What has taken place? We possibly may then understand what we are speaking of. There has been, and ever when the physical consciousness is at rest, the other self communes with the *soul* of the body, see? or it goes *out* into that realm of experience in the relationships of all experiences of that entity that may have been throughout the *eons* of time, or in correlating *with* that as it, that entity, *has* accepted as its criterion or standard of judgments, or justice, within its sphere of activity.

Hence through such an association in sleep there may have come that peace, that understanding, that is accorded by that which has been correlated through that passage of the selves of a body in sleep. Hence we find the more spiritual-minded individuals are the more easily pacified, at peace, harmony, in normal active state as well as in sleep. Why? They have set before themselves (Now we are speaking of one individual!) that that *is* a criterion that may be wholly relied upon, for that from which an entity or soul sprang is its *concept*, its awareness of, the divine or creative forces within their experience. Hence they that have named the Name of the Son have put their trust in Him. He their standard, their model, their hope, their activity. Hence we see how that the action through such sleep, or such quieting as to enter the silence—What do we mean by entering the silence? Entering the presence of that which *is* the criterion of the selves of an entity!

On the other hand oft we find one may retire with a feeling of elation, or peace, and awaken with a feeling of depression, of aloofness, of being alone, of being without hope, or of fear entering, and the *body-physical* awakes with that depression that manifests itself as of low spirits, as is termed, or of coldness, gooseflesh over the body, in expressions of the forces. What has taken place? A comparison in that "arms of Morpheus", in that silence, in that relationship of the physical self being unawares of those comparisons between the soul and its experiences of that period with the experiences of itself throughout the ages, and the experience may not have been remembered as a dream—but it lives *on*—and on, and must find its expression in the relationships of all it has experienced in whatever sphere of activity it may have found itself. Hence we find oft individual circumstances of where a spiritual-minded individual in the material plane (that is, to outward appearances of individuals so viewing same) suffering oft under pain, sickness, sorrow, and the like. What takes place? The experiences of the soul are meeting that which it has merited, for the clarification for the associations of itself with that whatever has been set as its ideal. If one has set self in array against that of love as manifested by the Creator, in its activity brought into material plane, then there *must* be a continual—continual—*warring* of those elements. By the comparison we may find, then, how it was that, that energy of creation manifested in the Son—by the activities of the Son in the material plane, could say "He sleeps", while to the outward eye it was death; for He *was*—and *is*—and ever will be—Life and Death in one; for as we find ourselves *in* His presence, that we have builded in the soul makes for that condemnation or that pleasing of the presence of that in His presence. So, my son, let thine lights be in Him, for these are the *manners* through which all may come to an understanding of the activities; for, as was given, "I was in the Spirit on the Lord's day." "I was caught up to the seventh heaven. Whether I was in the body or out of the body I cannot tell." What was taking place? The subjugation of the physical attributes in accord and attune with its infinite force as set as its ideal brought to that soul, "Well done, thou good and faithful servant, enter into the joys of thy Lord." "He that would be the greatest among you—" Not as the Gentiles, not as the heathen, not as the scribes or Pharisees, but "He that would be the greatest will be the *servant* of all."

What, then, has this to do—you ask—with the subject of sleep? Sleep—that period when the soul takes stock of that it has acted upon during one rest period to another, making or drawing—as it were—the comparisons that make for Life itself in its *essence*, as for harmony, peace, joy, love, long-suffering, patience, brotherly love, kindness—these are the fruits of the Spirit. Hate, harsh words, unkind thoughts, oppressions and the like, these are the fruits of the evil forces, or Satan and the soul either abhors that it has passed, or enters into the joy of its Lord. . . .

Reading 262–8

(Q) *After group meditation for the folks in New York, I dreamed I was talking to and walking with Gladys. She said, "They do not pay their rent." I asked who owned the place (we seemed near a house). Gladys said, "Mr. Cayce." The building seemed quite large and rambling and was at the Beach. We wandered around the place, and I noticed much iron rubbish, both old and new. Gladys seemed to fade out of the picture. I still wandered around the place, discovered a lovely lake, clear as crystal, beautiful white swans swimming around and being fed by loving happy children. Looking over the lake I saw there beautiful houses like a new settlement of beautiful happy homes, a white village, flowers, etc. Then I was so happy, felt uplifted, etc. What is the significance of this dream? [See 262-8, Par. R2.]*

(A) This, as is indicated, is emblematical of conditions within the development of the individual, or *entity*—individual itself, as to the individual ideal in that as is held in its consciousness. Now apply that as has been given, as to how the activities of a body–consciousness or mental body acts upon incidents or happenings in a material plane, and we will find the answers in the material sense; that is, *sense* conditions of material nature represent the spiritual or mental and spiritual aspects, and as the body viewed those of disorders, representing in the body–consciousness that of laxness, or inability in directions that made for disorders; yet as these are turned into directions that become of more the mental and spiritual aspect, the visions of that as would *again* be held by the *entity*, or *individual*, as ideal, or idealistic, arise from the rubbish of those things material. *Dreams* are such of which buildings come into the material aspects of life. First as visions that are as to some visionary, unreal. They are crystallized in the lives and activities of others through those constant actions upon the various elements in the body of an individual entity, which is as being studied. Then they act upon those in such a manner as to bring into being realities, that in a material plane represent those; as the peace and tranquility of the lake with its crystal fountains, and the swans as representing peace and serenity as come with such surroundings, and with the *hope* as in flowers and blossoms and children. Then the whole as *emblems* in the body–consciousness, seeing, visioning, that to which its own self *is* raising, *may* raise, those *around* self. Hence the entity, the body, *truly* the missionary, the emissary.

Reading 136–33

(Q) *I saw an animal crawling over the ground, just sort of semi-conscious, in a condition of half gray dawn.*

(A) This is as the entity itself awakening to that consciousness of the indwelling of that spirit that beareth witness to the truth of the indwelling of the spirit of that One that gives and takes, and gives and takes, that we may become One with Him.

(Q) *Is this some awakening—of what and who?*

(A) Apply to self, [136].

Reading 2218–1

(Q) *Regarding the dream—[. . .], my son, kept telling me something—impressing upon me most forcibly not to forget it, but upon awakening I had. Another time, [. . .] was telling me something, and was also saying, whatever I did to not let Mr. [. . .] hear what he had said.*

(A) In this respect, as has been intimated and given the body may gain much of an understanding as respecting mental, material, and spiritual conditions, Dreams are of three characters, or natures: Those that are of the purely physical, wherein conditions are magnified through the action of the digestive system, and are often called nightmares. In that of the purely mental aberration, or imagination, these have often been designated as suppressed desires, or of those natures innate wherein the self, or the *entity*—the soul of self—attempts to reason with the purely mental mind. Then there is that condition as has been presented to this body, in that the cosmic forces of the universal force, in which those who have passed from the material or physical plane may attune their selves, their souls, to the *mind* of the soul of an individual who has that force in self where in the material is laid aside. Then we find these as here given, that the physical or material is only able to bring that portion to self's consciousness where the individual impressed self upon the activity of the mental force of self. These may be applied in the material sense, either as warnings or as knowledge, or as understanding, and in each may gain that of the assistance of the broader vision of the individual who thus effects the communicating force, or element between same. In these—that as is given in the body was *not* to forget referring to those promises the body often made, that the self would ever remain with the body—absent from *body*, yet in soul and spirit ever present. In that *warning* as *given, that as* a warning to protect the body. Cultivate an understanding—apply that known—and more may be given.

Reading 281-19

(Q) [993]: *Please interpret the following dream which I received a few days before Christmas: I was climbing a ladder and as I approached the top I became conscious of one round being out of ladder at the top. It was with great difficulty that I continued the climb at this point. Thankful to say, I was able with my fingertips to reach the top. It took all my strength to pull my body up. Those who were following back of me seemed to have no such difficulty, and one of the group made that remark. There was an answer by one already there, that as I made the climb I had laid the last round in the ladder.*

(A) Both prophetic and profound in *this* experience of the body–consciousness with the soul's experience. That the ladder represents the Way is evidenced, as has been given in interpretations for those that visioned even the ladder to heaven upon which there ascended and descended the angels of light. In that the rung was missing and that self had to make the effort to attain the top makes for those experiences oft in the mind's consciousness of many, that others that self considers as having an easy way do not become confronted with those hardships as, as is felt at times, are experienced by others. But rather as the voice that came from above, when the self had made the way easier for those that would ascend by the experiences of self, that "I *am* the way," knowing that He made of Himself no estate that others *through* Him might have the access to the Father. And as the voice of those who cry the way is easier that thou hast made the last rung, for us; and as there is the cry from above, "Well done," there should come that peace within self that thine work of thine hand is acceptable in His sight. Be not unto vainglory, but rather in that happiness that passeth understanding in knowing that the work of thine hands is acceptable in His sight.

Reading 39-3

MHB: Now you will have before you the body of [39], present in this room, and the enquiring mind of this body, who had the dream I will give you during the course of the past six years. At various times during the past six years the body has experienced the following: Visualized airship heavier than air, which collects its lifting and driving force from the atmosphere by means of points on the top of it. Underneath this machine there are apparently two heavy copper bars running the length of it, having small points underneath, which when charged with the force lifts the machine from the air apparently neutralizing the force of gravity. The machine was driven by the power streaming from points attached to the rear. You will give the interpretation of this dream or vision, tell us if such a machine is practical and if such a power is available, and how such may be made. You will answer questions regarding this.

EC: Yes, we have the body, the enquiring mind, [39], here. With dreams and visions as come to individual, these are of various classes and groups, and are the emanations from the conscious, subconscious, or superconscious, or the combination and correlation of each, depending upon the individual and the personal development of the individual, and are to be used in the lives of such for the betterment of such individual.

In this vision, we find this emblematical condition being presented to the entity. Not wholly a condition that may not be made feasible, plausible, workable, or used in the operation of man's endeavor; yet to the entity is as an emblematical condition, with those of the conscious forces using that which the mind has dwelt upon to show the higher forces as are to be used by the entity in the spiritual, mental, and physical development for same and as we see in the various presentations of the vision, the slight changes that occur in the make-up of the machine show the various amount of endeavor within the mental forces of the entity to gain the understanding of same; for, as is seen, there will appear this same vision three other periods in the development of the entity, and in each there will be seen again changes as are to come in the entity's understanding of the emanations, or the abilities of individuals to apply in the life of an entity in material plane the various lessons as are attained or gained from same. As is seen, all of the power must come from above. The bars representing, then, as the individual's foundation, upon which there is given the lifting power of same to soar through the various fields of knowledge in attaining the various points necessary for that development and that understanding to apply such forces in the material plane. Just as is seen in the various points from the machine, shows that all force, while as of one, is gained through the various sources and contacts as are made, and is called in the material plane that of the environmental forces, while in that of the hereditary forces is as that left in the wake of the impelling force that drives the body and the mind through those spaces necessary to make the individual one in all of its applications in the various fields of endeavor, whether studying the higher fields of thought or in making the turns or curves in the various walks of life, and in the individuals as the entity contacts from time to time.

In the application of same as from the field of the purely mechanical forces, these—as they are presented from time to time—will bring to the knowledge of the individual that as is necessary to bring about the changes in mechanical appliance of that force known as the earth-side force as has been applied in eons ago to those crafts that soared through the ether. [See Life reading 39-2.]

Be satisfied with that attained from the experience, until there is through a little here, a little there, line upon line, precept upon precept—applying that already gained, that more may be given unto thee.

Ready for questions.

(Q) *The entity, then, may seek this source for further information on coming experiences?*

(A) The entity may seek all sources—for, as is seen, there are many points toward the heavens, as of the lifting power. The stability of self—as is set in those bars that lift or parallel with the earth—must be kept in that brightness as is seen, that there may be attained more power, more force, in the applying in self that already attained.

(Q) *That is all of the questions in this reading.*

(A) We are through with this reading for the present for much may be given to the entity as respecting its (the entity's) development, mentally, spiritually, physically.

Use that in hand—for the simple rod stretched over the mighty sea became the power in the hands of him who walked with the Creative Energy—God. The withered rod became the budded almond in the hands of him who sought to know His ways, and applied same in the life. Keep thine paths straight. Walk in the shadow of His wing. Keep thine eyes, thine heart, ever to that source from which emanates all power that lifts man toward the Creator.

Reading 137–84

(Q) *I was going in bathing in the ocean surf and started to dive into a breaker, but instead found that I dived head first right into the sand and was caught there head first. [140] called to [4167] to help and they tried to pull me out. I woke up trying to breathe, but was having great difficulty and feeling that I was suffocating from my experience in the sand.*

(A) This again is as an experience to this body–conscious mind, of this individual, [137], of the various conditions and phases as are taking place in the mind of the entity.

As is seen, the ocean represents that as to which all life in the material or physical plane proceeds, in its way and manner. The sand is the basis of the thing. Diving head first, then, into, as it were, the ocean of experience, the entity may find self fast in same, and such a mind as that as is called upon, by one close to the entity, to assist or relieve same, may confuse the mind as to that which it has obtained in its diving into sea of experience of the entity's existence in the material and spiritual plane, and thus bring consternation, or, as is seen from the physical existence, that trouble in gaining or keeping its mental equilibrium in this condition or this sea of experience. See?

This, then, is as a lesson to the entity, that in the taking on of that experience that the entity sees, knows, understands, grasps a portion of, in the various phases of its earthly or physical or material existence, the lessons are then as stepping–stones, and *wade* in, rather than dive in head first. For little by little, line upon line, line upon line, must one gain the full concept of the conditions in which one lives, moves, and has its being. Not that life and its phases are a mystery, or something to be afraid of, but rather that the glory of the knowing *of* the existence and its *meaning* is the worth while condition in the material and the spiritual spheres and planes; for, as is experienced in the entity's own concept, in the days as they pass, with fear for the physical conditions of the body, for the mental urges of the body, with the various phases of

the material conditions, with the various phases of the mental development, there comes to the entity those awakenings, in those various conditions as transpire within the entity's own self, in the vibrations that
are felt about the body, and the wonder comes—are these vibrations as
are experienced of the material making, or are they the presence of
some unseen force from within that would find expression in the world,
or are they from unseen forces in another plane that seek a manner of
expression in this plane?

Then, as is seen and known of the entity, from these experiences that
are given here, these are as but one. Fear not! *Wade* in! Don't dive in!
Meet the conditions, and be ever ready, as was with those of old—"Here
am I! Use me!"

Reading 262-9

(Q) *[288]: Is the interpretation and lesson correct, which I have written on the
vision presented through me on the morning of Jan. 9, '32?*

([288]'s vision of Saturday morning, January 9, 1932—about 6:30
o'clock.] I appeared in the midst of a group of people, packed close
together, standing, dressed in white and blindfolded. Each one was trying to take off their bandage and put it on someone else. Just having
arrived, I did not have a bandage over my eyes—and realized that they
were all approaching me with the intention of putting one on me. Reasoning with myself, I knew that if I resisted them they would overcome
me by their great number. So I withdrew myself mentally, closed my
eyes and separated myself mentally from them, at the same time saying
the little prayer on Knowing Self. As I did so, I used my hands as wings
and slowly began to rise. The others were prevented from touching me
by my state of consciousness. As my feet rose a little above their heads,
I could see them clamoring and reaching, trying to catch hold of my
feet. I rose higher and higher, getting lighter and lighter, and it became
easier and easier for me to transcend space. As I passed through each
plane of development my form changed, and I became transparent.
Finally I reached my goal and stopped moving. I was a round ball, and
reminded myself very much of the full moon—as it looks to us from the
earth. I could see myself and feel myself—my consciousness was in me
(the ball), all around, and everywhere. Then I *melted*—evaporated, the

same as smoke or a cloud, and became one with and a part of the whole universe. The most wonderful, pleasurable, and *all-inclusive* feeling came through me that I have ever experienced. (It is impossible to put it into words.)

(A) In part, correct. Better, in the interpreting of vision, that is evident in itself of being emblematical, that there be sufficient of collaborations of events as *is* affecting individuals seen. Then a more nearer the interpretation may be had.

(Q) *What is the deeper significance of this dream?*

(A) Better wait and see! [See above dream.]

Reading 900–64

(Q) *April 25, 1925: It seemed there were two ways of crossing a river, the upper bridge and the lower. As some others used lower one, so did I but this time was lying down and traveling right along the water's edge. It seemed dangerous to me, yet had been done so often before I had full confidence.*

(A) In this we find that correlation of the physical and the subconscious forces is given, and the lessons as gotten here: The river the way of life, the passage over the existence or span through or over which the material man passes in the passage through earth's plane. There are two ways, the higher and the lower way. That in the higher giving the great broad outlook over the whole of Universal Forces, that of the lower in ever the way of the great masses. "Choose thou as to whom thou will serve."

Reading 341–15

(Q) *Night of 25, or morning of 26 of October, 1925. Dreamed of riding with someone to the top of a high mountain. Then they showed me a beautiful view spread out below. They said something—Recall—*

(A) This as seen indicates the emblematical conditions being carried in the mental forces of entity and correlated through cosmic conditions that as is the interpretation of the vision or dream seen and experienced. As is seen, to the high mountain is that as the life in its development to those conditions that give the more perfect understanding of the physical world. The view as obtained, being, then, as entity in possession of knowledge to acquire possessions, or to gain those of the proclivities of the physical world in that way and manner in which the world becomes, as it were, the dross to the mental forces of the entity, for as is seen in that as said, "Though beautiful—and one gain the whole world and lose his own soul, what is the gain therein?"

Reading 294-15

Editor's Note: This is one of Edgar Cayce's own dreams.

Background of Reading 294-15

Background information preceding [Reading] 294-15 as told to those gathered to hear the reading on 1/13/25:

My last experience with a return of ophonia was possibly the most noteworthy. I do not know as I yet understand its whole import. This was the experience: [12/19/19]

For about 10 days I had been unable to speak above a whisper. I felt that if I were able to get myself in the subconscious state, possibly I could through that means again find relief. It was Sunday afternoon. My wife sent the older boy for a walk and ride with the younger boy, who was then a very small baby. We retired to the bedroom; where I proceeded to put myself into the unconscious state.

The experience lasted possibly 30 minutes, and it is the only one where I have been able to recall anything that transpired. There have been quite a number of times when I have had dreams while in such a state. Was this a dream?

Scene 1: Apparently, there was spread before me all the graveyards in the world. I saw nothing save the abode of what we call the dead, in all portions of the world.

Scene 2: Then, as the scene shifted, the graves seemed to be centered around India, and I was told by a voice from somewhere, 'Here you will know a man's religion by the manner in which his body has been disposed of.' [See 275-29, Par. 22-A, on 12/21/32.]

Scene 3: The scene then changed to France, and I saw the soldiers' graves, and among them the grave of 3 boys who had been in my S.S. class. Then I saw the boys, not dead but alive. Each of them told me how they met their death; one in machine gun fire, another, in the bursting of a shell, the other in the heavy artillery fire. Two gave me messages to tell their loved ones at home. They appeared much in the same way and manner as they did the day each came to bid me good-bye.

Scene 4: As the scene changed again, I apparently reasoned with myself, 'This is what men call spiritualism. Can it be true? Are all those we call dead yet alive in some other plane of experience or existence? Could I see my own baby boy?' [Milton Porter Cayce]

As if a canopy was raised, tier on tier of babies appeared. In the 3rd or 4th row from the top, to the side, I recognized my own child. He knew me, even as I knew him. He smiled his recognition, but no word of any kind passed.

Scene 5: The scene changed, and there appeared a lady friend who was being buried in the local cemetery during that selfsame hour, one whom I had known very well and from whom I had purchased many flowers for distribution by the children in my S.S. classes. She talked with me about the changes that men call death, said that it was a real birth. Especially she spoke concerning the effect the gift of flowers had upon individuals, and how they should be given in life rather than at funerals or death. As to what they meant, and how they spoke to the invalid, the shut-ins, and meant so little to those that had passed from material to the spiritual plane. Then she said, 'But to be material for the moment, some months ago someone left $2.50 with you for me. You are not aware of this having been done, and will find it in a drawer of your desk marked with the date it was paid, Aug. 8th, and there are 2 paper dollars with a 50 cent piece. See that my daughter receives this, for she will need it. Be patient with the children, they are gaining much.'

Scene 6: Again the scene changed, and there appeared a man [4971] who had been a fellow officer for years in the church of which I was a member. He spoke of his son [228], who was a very close friend of mine, but was soon to return from the army, saying that he would no doubt return to his place in the local bank but advising that he rather accept the offer which would be made from a moving picture house. Then he spoke concerning the affairs of the church, and then I was physically conscious again.

When I awoke my voice was all right, I could talk normally, though my wife told me I had said not a word during the whole 30 minutes. I told her immediately about the experience.

In re Scene 5: I went to my office and looked in the drawer of the desk where I was told to look and sure enough there was the envelope that had been received on the 8th of August by one of the young ladies who had since left the studio (and this was in December).

In re Scene 6: The next day I had occasion to go to the bank and the young man, my friend, took my deposit. I asked when he returned, and he said last night. I asked if he expected to remain in the bank and he said he thought so. Then I told him I had something I would like to relate to him, and that he could act as he felt right. He came to the studio within the hour, and I related to him the whole experience. He told me that on his way home from Washington he had stopped in Atlanta, that he had been approached by a friend and asked to take the management of a moving picture theatre, but he had that morning mailed him a letter rejecting the offer, but that he would immediately wire him accepting it—which he did.

What this experience meant, I do not know, whether I have the whole interpretation.

In re scenes 1 through 4: This one thing I do know. I have traveled in many portions of the country, north, south, east and west. There are few, if any, cemeteries, that do not appear familiar, so much so yet that when I see even a corner of one I can with a few minutes reflection tell many intimate things about that particular cemetery.

What was it? I do not know.

Reading 294–15

MHB: You will have before you the body of Edgar Cayce, present in this room, and the vision [Dream 1] this body had, in the psychic condition, on Sunday afternoon, December 19, 1919.

You will also have before you the dream [Dream 2] recently had by this body regarding Mr. Linden Shroyer, the water running over the rocks, and separating the people in groups, and seemingly illustrating the character of the peoples by that surrounding the individual group, trying to catch the fish, which broke, and the effort to put same together again.

You will also have before you the dream [Dream 3] had by this body, Edgar Cayce, Monday, Jan. 5, 1925, regarding the association of the body,

Edgar Cayce, in work of the Institute, with the body, Morton Blumenthal, and the body Madison Byron Wyrick. You will interpret each one of these three dreams, and tell us what lessons we may gain from them.

EC: Yes, we have the body here, and the vision and dream as was had by this body at the times given.

As we see, all visions and dreams are given for the benefit of the individual, [if they would] would they but interpret them correctly, for we find that visions, or dreams, in whatever character they may come, are the reflection, either of the physical condition, with apparitions with same, or of the subconscious, with the conditions relating to the physical body and its action, either through mental or through the elements of the spiritual entity, or a projection from the spiritual forces to the subconscious of the individual, and happy may he be that is able to say they have been spoken to through the dream or vision.

In these as given, we find in the first . . . [Dream 1] the vision of the existent condition in the physical plane, and this given in the emblematical way that should remove all doubt of any character regarding the material, the elemental of the mental and the spiritual plane.

In the first [Dream 1, Scene 1], we find the representation of a waiting world; all still, all dead, and as has been given, the day will come when those in the grave will have the gospel preached unto them. [John 5:25. . .]

In the separation of the dead [Scene 2], and the showing of the religions of the world represented in one place, [India] we find exemplifying the need of awakening.

In the graves of France [Scene 3], that of the work [of Edgar Cayce?] begun, for we find those relations that existed in a material world projected from the spiritual world.

In that of the body finding the vision of the offspring of the material body [Scene 4], in the realm of the spiritual plane, this again showing that recognition from the spiritual plane of condition existent in a material world, or plane.

In that just passed into the realm of the spiritual plane [Scene 5], and represented by the fruits of the manifestation of love, thought, these show how the correlation of thought and deed in the material world may act upon those just entered in the spiritual plane, and not receded from the earth's plane.

In the last [Scene 6], the thought of the ability of those that are in the mental forces held close, which lend of their spiritual force in an earth plane, though receded from the earthbound conditions. . . .

This for the [12/19/19] vision. . . .

In the dream of the water . . . [Dream 2] with the separating of the acquaintance [Linden Shroyer, etc.] of the body, we find the manifestation again in the subconscious forces of the water, representing the life, the living way, that separates those of every walk of life and about each entity, or group, there is builded that which radiates in an earth's sphere, or in a spiritual sphere that of the deeds done in the body.

In the representing of the fish, which is the representation of Him, who became the Living Way, the Water of Life, given for the healing of all nations, and in the breaking, and in the separation, yet will there be brought the force that will *f*again make this the Living Way, the perfect representation of the force necessary to give the life to all.

In this of the condition . . . [Dream 3] regarding the material forces, necessary for the material manifestation of work on the earth plane given as a way, which many groups, through two individuals [Morton H. Blumenthal and Madison Byron Wyrick], may work out that necessary for the performance of much given in the vision and dream.

(Q) What is meant . . . [Dream 1, Scene 1] by those in the grave shall have the gospel preached to them?

(A) That same condition as we see manifest through the spiritual entity again having that work presented in the earth plane, that they, the entity, may accept, or reject, that gospel.

(Q) Where do entities recede to . . . [Dream 1, Scene 6] after leaving earth's plane?

(A) As was given, in that "Touch not, for I have not yet ascended unto my Father." [John 20:17] In the separation of the soul and spirit from an earthly abode, each enter the spirit realm. When the entity has fully completed its separation, it goes to that force through which the entity merits in the action upon the earth's plane, and in the various spheres, or in the various elements, as has been prepared for its (the spiritual entity) development, so the sojourn is taken, until the entity is ready for again manifesting through the flesh that development attained in the spiritual entity, for the will *must* be made one with the Father, that we may enter into that realm of the blessed, for, as has been given [Matthew 5:8], only the true, the perfect, may see God [Hebrews 12:14], and we *must* be one with Him.

Reading 281-6

(Q) What is the meaning of the dream I had regarding being handed a cup and spoon, and feeding people with spiritual food?

(A) As indicated, that it is necessary for much of that which may be given or measured out be in small doses, and not in a manner that would cause the individuals to become antagonistic to that which would be as truth. Know ye, no one finite mind may have all the truth!

5

●

Communication with the Dead in Dreams

Editor's Note: As Elsie Sechrist notes, "The dead differ from the living only in this respect: they are in a permanently subconscious state because the conscious mind of the physical body no longer exists. But the body is an expendable shell, and all else is intact. On the astral level of existence, the subconscious mind replaces the conscious mind of the soul, and the superconscious replaces the subconscious."

Reading 243–5

Editor's Note: A point often stressed in the Cayce readings is that contact with the dead has as its first purpose a transformation and quickening of the dreamer.

MHB: You will have before you the body and enquiring mind of [243], present in this room, and the dream this body had of recent date, in which her [deceased] mother, [3776], came to her and put her arms around her, and told her that she loved her. The body asked her if she knew how much she had always loved her, and the mother replied, "Yes, you've proven it always."

EC: Yes, we have the body and the enquiring mind of this body, [243], present in this room.

The dreams, as we see, come to individuals through the subjugation of the conscious mind, and the subconscious being of the soul—when loosed—is able to communicate with the subconscious minds of those whether in the material or the cosmic plane. In this as is seen the body-mind takes that concept of the subconscious that is closest to the soul forces of the body, and the mother in the living being as it is, then, gives that assurance to the body through this means of its full life existence:

"Sister—Sister—as is seen by you, Mother sees, Mother knows, Mother feels those same feelings of that love which is in the earth that makes of the heavenly home. And while I am in the spirit planes I am yet present in the minds and hearts of those who express to me the love as builded in the being—the love the Master shows to all when He gave that He would prepare the home for those who would come after Him.

"Love those about you in the way that Mother gave, and be that as Mother would have you be—for Mother does not leave you, Sister—and Mother knows! for the life is the whole life, even as the Master gave that He was the life and the light of the world, in that same concept as shown in that felt as Mother gathers Sister in her arms—and Mother knows! Mother Knows!" [GD's noted: Her mother's pet name for her was "Sister."]

(Q) *The mother guides, guards, as the living angel, though unseen to sensuous eyes?*

(A) In this there is seen that as has oft been given, that through the subjugation of physical forces the subconscious—which is the mind of the soul—communicates those same feelings, those same expressions, which are that which really builds in the material plane—for as is experienced by this body-conscious mind, [243], there is seen the love that is expressed through the mother love. *Not* as that which is passed, or gone, or not present, or not among the living! for *God* is God of the living, the Savior is the Savior of the living. Let him that is dead bury the dead. Let him that is alive be alive to that which may be gained by those closer manifestations of the guards that keep those who seek to know His way.

Reading 136–70

(Q) *That of August 29th or 30th. Both my [deceased mother [139] and father appeared to me, and were so glad to see me. They told me about [3816] my sister, that she committed suicide, or killed herself.*

(A) This is the manner presents to the entity, or to the body—consciousness, the mother and father giving to this body the understanding of the working, as it were, of the mind of the sister, and the inept way, or the inability of that body to give that correct application to the conditions in the life that satisfies same. And—as is seen—the bodies (the ethereal body or astral body) depend upon the physical body here, [136], to so instruct, to so direct, to so counsel the body—[3816] the sister—in the way and manner that the better understanding, and that the growth in the spiritual sense, may come to the body, rather than those of the nature that bring deterioration to the development of the body, see? for these conditions are held in the mind. Remembering, then, thoughts are deeds in the spiritual sense, for they make or mar the actions of inner being . . .

(Q) *Morning of August 25th, regarding my mother [139] and her pointing out a crowd to me, about Sidney [. . .] who lay dying. He was in the last stage of the process. I saw his eyes glazed. My [deceased] mother seemed to call attention to this. Then in a final effort he tried to get up. Those about him would not permit. My mother showed me that of course they would not. Then he dropped back and died. I cried, at which my mother instructed me not to cry.*

(A) In this emblematical way and manner we find there are lessons being given to this body through the efforts of the mother or the guardian forces for this body, those lessons as pertain to the various phases of development in life. In this particular individual as seen, and as understood by the mother, this entity represents a definite condition in the physical affairs, or in certain social positions and standings. In the death there is seen this representing that in the meeting of same all become of one level. And in the attempt at such period there is naught that may be done to change those conditions which surround an individual life. And then the lesson being—that the will in man, or woman, is that factor that is to be used for the betterment of the development in and through this material plane. While there may be the positions, those conditions that are of the flesh or of the earth-earthy that satisfy for the time being; yet these do not answer. Neither do they give that better understanding, nor that peace that comes with the life *well* lived and in service to others.

In the lessons then as gained, apply same in self's own life. Not as that which would cause dissension, discussion, or any condition that would bring adverse criticism to self. Neither put on the long face nor think that there is aught but the dream of the future. Life is real, life is earnest! yet it is not all of life to live, nor all of death to die—for with the thoughts and the deeds done in the mind and the body, these are that builded by the entity, or body, and must be met, and an account given of those things rendered in the body and the mind. For the soul liveth, and is a portion of the Creative Energy, and it returns to the Whole, yet reserving in itself the oneness in the ability to know itself individual, yet a portion of the Whole. What manner of man would one be that would make of that Whole its own concept, other than one with the Whole?

Reading 140-10

(Q) Next, [137], my mother and myself were sitting in a room, I in my blue wrapper. I knew I was dead, yet there I was seated just as I do today, dressed and looking the same as in physical life and I was wondering if anyone knew that I was there, if they knew what I knew—that I had been killed. I could see them and myself, but could they see me—know I was sitting there and also know that I myself, even though dead, knew of my own presence—of my own consciousness? I was sitting next to [137] caressing him—loving him just the same as before. Just then my Aunt Lily [. . .] came into the room and spoke to my mother and [137]. Now I realized that this would be my proof as to whether they knew of my presence or not. Aunt Lily [. . .] looked directly at the chair upon which I was seated, but she did not see me—to her I was not there!

(A) This again shows that same force as given in that concept of the preparation necessary in the physical that each may understand that connection which lies between the physical and the spiritual, that such a condition as viewed and experienced by the entity in this vision may be in that way and manner as to be able to bridge this chasm. That is, that the consciousness of this entity is gaining in this vision a concept of what is called physical death, and that the consciousness, with all its earthly ties, so long as it (that consciousness) remains in the earth's plane, it (that consciousness) is cognizant of that condition taking place in the physical, see? and is then the spiritual action. Then the lesson is as given. The entity should gain from this that concept of the great truths which are gained from the subconscious forces which are being manifest in the physical world, that the full consciousness of self's projection from the subconscious, or death plane, may even be understood, comprehended, in the physical.

(Q) *I was dead, yet conscious of myself as [140], dressed as she dressed, in the same room as [140] lived in. Would this be possible to the spirit entity of [140] in elemental form? Would I in form be able to do that?*

(A) The consciousness of the subconscious is of the earthly in the death plane, as the spiritual consciousness is in the physical plane. One projects into the other as the other projects from one to the other. And as there is seen manifest in the physical plane those actions of the spiritual force, so may there be in the spiritual elemental plane that action into the physical plane, see? and the projection then is of that same force brought by that seen that brings this entity in this condition—the love, the affection, the desire of that nearness, of that oneness with those individuals as seen, see?

(Q) *Would this cosmic consciousness be possible to my subconscious consciousness—the consciousness of the life after death?*

(A) As given.

(Q) *Would I retain my love for my husband and could I be conscious of myself caressing him?*

(A) Just in the way and manner as given, see? for as is seen, let's give this as an illustration of how the cosmic consciousness, or elemental consciousness, after death projects from one to the other, see? The loved one—just reverse the condition, see? The loved one is in the spiritual plane. The one as the lover is putting self in that attunement with that spiritual love element, as is manifest in physical or material forces. Then, that love brings each to the arms, as it were, of the other, see?

(Q) *Could I not only see the spirit reality with my new spirit mind, but also see the phenomenized form of this spirit in the physical bodies of my mother, my husband, my Aunt Lily?*

(A) Just as has been explained and given, see?

(Q) *Would it be my choice as to whether I desired to return to these conditions— say of love for my husband or not? Having created the faculty of love for this individual, could I take the old form of [140], come to [137] and caress him?*

(A) With the attunement from the other, as given, see?

(Q) *As shown here, the physical [137] would not know of this—but could he know of it if he went to sleep—i.e. his subconsciousness and my subconsciousness meet as a vibration force meets a radio machine and causes a sound when the machine is tuned in?*

(A) Just as given. This is the illustration, see? Both must be in that attunement and separated from the physical forces to become conscious, for these are of the spiritual elements.

(Q) *If this is so, could I deliver a message to [140] or my mother? Then why could not I deliver a message through another mind, another channel that I might find, to convey a message to [137].*

(A) Only with an attunement is the message received, as in the radio. Only with the same attunement may a message be delivered to an individual, see?

(Q) *In this case, then, ones who subjugated their physical selves, (mediums—so called) would be channels for such a message—would open themselves to the operation of such messages being sent from my dead self to my living husband? Is this so?*

(A) Much as a kiss may be *sent* from one individual to another.

(Q) *That is, the subconscious of a medium might find in the one spirit subconscious condition my love condition and express it, if his physical or another physical caused the medium's subconsciousness to tune into love thoughts. Correct?*

(A) Only correct as has been explained before in regards this, for the medium is as but that through which the transmission of a condition passes or exists, and is wavered by that physical, by that cosmic consciousness of that individual; while (get the difference, see?) a subconscious condition in which the subconscious contacts by suggestion the whole one spirit force that is, as an element of existent force in nature, and in the condition, the presentation of the fact—is manifested according to abilities of the entity to present same to the consciousness of the individual desiring that information from that cosmic consciousness, see? You don't see but this is it, see?

(Q) *Now, bringing this into an example: If [137] by, or my mother directed by, physical thought or word their own or someone else's subconsciousness to attunement with my subconscious spirit action of love.*

(A) (EC interrupting) By themselves they may, *but not through someone else*, gain that close access to that consciousness of the nearness and at-oneness of the individual, see?

(Q) (Continuing) [137] or my mother could receive through their own subconscious channel or the same subconscious channel in the medium.

(A) (EC again interrupting) Not in the medium—in Self. Leave out the medium if you would understand these conditions!

(Q) (Continuing) could receive the love action in my subconscious consciousness expressed in words of their comprehension? Correct?

(A) Correct only as has been given! Forget these!

Reading 136-45

(Q) Morning of September 5. My [deceased] mother appeared to me. She said to me: "I am alive."

(A) (Interrupting) She is alive!

(Q) (Continuing) "Something is wrong with your sister's leg, or shoulder." (or both—I don't clearly remember) "She ought see a doctor about it."

(A) This, as is seen, to the entity, is that experience drawing closer and closer to that at-oneness with the spiritual forces manifest through the at-onement of the forces manifested in this material plane. For, as is seen, the mother, through the entity's own mind, is as the mother to all in that household. Warning, then, of conditions that may arise, and of conditions existent. Then, warn the sister as regarding same, see?

(Q) Now here is a definite proof—that if my mother can tell me that something is the matter with my sister and of which trouble I am ignorant, then I must conclude—

(A) (interrupting) Then the body is ignorant only in the physical sense. The subconscious is in at-onement with the mother and the sister, in the subconscious state, see? Understand these conditions, as the entity attempts to gain the lesson that is being given.

Reading 136-33

GC: You will have before you the body and the enquiring mind of [136] of New York City, and the dreams this body had on the dates which I will give you. You will give the interpretation and lesson to be gained from each of these, as I read same to you, and you will answer the questions which I ask you regarding same:

EC: Yes, we have the body here, with the enquiring mind of same. This we have had before.

The dreams as we see which come to the body are for the edification of the mental forces of the body, and when used aright these may give the entity the better understanding of the phenomena of life, and of how same, in its various forms and manners, are manifested in the spiritual and physical world, and how the physical may become cognizant of same. Ready for dreams.

(Q) *Night of Saturday, February 13, or Sunday morning, February 14, 1926. I heard a voice that I recognized as J.S.'s, our old friend from New Orleans, who loved me dearly as a child, yet whom I have not seen in 2 to 3 years. The impression of J.S. talking to me was very pronounced, and for a while I did not see her figure, yet I felt that she was with Mother at the hospital, as mother changed from this earthly consciousness to the other. J.S. was there as the transition was made—was now with Mother as she said to me:* "your mother is as happy as ever—" *More J.S. told me about Mother which I can't remember. Recall and explain to me, please.*

(A) In this there is given to the entity that understanding of what is meant by the life other than the physical. For, as it is seen that the companionship of loved ones seek the companionship in that plane, for "As a tree falls so shall it lie," there is seen the message coming from the loved one to the one regarding the loved one, showing then that companionship, that without the loss of the care of others, as is seen.

Then, the entity should gain that strength from that given regarding the condition, and know that the mother lives in that realm in which there is recognized J. S., and that the companionship is there, until those developments come from the earth plane to lead on to those higher realms, or to come again. For those many changes must come to each and every entity in its development. And as these are seen, then, the strength, the understanding, should be gained by this entity. For as is given, she is *well, happy, and free* from the care as is given in earth's plane, yet with that same love as is raised through the companionship with the oneness of the spiritual forces with the soul, see?

(Q) *I was not thinking of J.S. who died 3 weeks before Mother—how and why did this entity transmit the message to me?*

(A) As is seen, the entity may answer same from within self, if the entity would not condemn self for physical conditions, for this brings the sorrow in the heart, physical self-condemnation toward conditions existent. Then, when this is laid aside, there may be seen how that the friendship, the love of one close, near and dear, is ready to give that aid, when one attunes self to that position, condition, wherein one, the entity, may gain from each and every experience to bring self to that better understanding of that phenomenized force in the physical world. See? For, as is seen then in this presented, that the entity may know, *not alone* does the mother go out; not alone in that unseen world, yet with that same care, that same love, raised to a better *understanding* of the forces as are manifested.

(Q) *Was J.S. there to guide Mother over the transition from physical to spiritual? Both died within 3 weeks—both must easily have yet been—be in this plane as yet— is this so?*

(A) Both in physical plane or earth's sphere as yet, until that force leads on in its ever developing toward that Oneness with the All Force, see?

(Q) *Then, does one spirit guide another over?*

(A) "Lo! I am with thee, and though I walk through the valley of the shadow of death, my spirit shall guide thee." As is seen in this, these are given in this manner that those may see, those may know, through that experience of such earthly partings, that is the lack of an understanding of that spiritual consciousness that prevents these forces from manifesting in the physical sense.

(Q) *Voice: "Your Mother is alive and happy."*

(A) Your mother is alive and happy. Just as is given, the entity may know that all force goes to show, to prove, to bring to the consciousness of the entity, that through that as ye *live* in Him ye shall be made *alive* in Him! for there is no death, only the transition from the physical to the spiritual plane. Then, as the birth into the physical is given as the time of the new life, just so, then, in physical is the birth into the spiritual.

(Q) *Then, does my mother see me and love me as ever?*

(A) Sees thee and loves thee as ever. Just as those forces were manifest in the physical world, and the entity entertains and desires and places self in that attunement with those desires of that entity, the love exists, in that far, in that manner, see? for in spirit all sham is laid aside.

(Q) *Does she try to tell me "I am alive and happy?"*

(A) *Tells* the entity "I am alive and happy" when entity will *attune* self to that at-oneness.

(Q) *I feel her with me, particularly as I kissed her clay body—I felt she knew and responded—but did she, or do I fool myself?*

(A) In that manner that entity poured out self to that entity, the response came. No, not fooling self, for the *soul* liveth, and is at peace, and would that this entity know that it liveth. And as has been given, "In my Father's house are many mansions, were it not so I would have told you," and "I go to prepare a place for you, that where *I am* there *ye* may be also." This is as applicable to the entity in this hour as was given by the Redeemer to those gathered about Him.

For as we entities in the physical plane prepare that at–oneness, it is as He gave: "Even as I be lifted up will draw all men unto me," or has been given, when speaking to those that would seek His face, "Say not to thyself who shall descend into the depths to bring Him up, or who shall fly into the heavens to bring Him down, for the spirit of peace, truth, and love, is *within thine own heart.*" As the spirit of self gives that attunement that may be at a oneness with those spirits in that sphere, they may know, they may understand, they may gather, that *truth* that *makes* one free.

(Q) My old beau, J.S., came to our house (New Orleans) to see me in my grief at the loss of my mother. He said to me: "I just came to see you because I loved your mother so."

(A) Again that presentation to the entity from the physical standpoint of how that love rules, guides, directs, the world; as is said, "God is Love," and as these physical beings give manifestations of that desire to comfort, cherish, for the love held in physical, so may the physical being understand the love held for the souls of those who love the Lord and His coming.

(Q) Then what does this indicate in relation to past events as related—

(A) (EC breaking in) That just as has been given. Not to the past but to the *present* conditions, and as this becomes, and is, as a beautiful tribute in the mind of the entity, to *self* and to the loved one, then let this be as the *lesson* to the entity: If the filial love is shown in the *material* world in such a manner, how much *greater* must be that love expressed by the Father in Heaven!

Report on Reading 294–114

Editor's Note: This is a dream of Edgar Cayce's that was not submitted for an interpretation in a reading.

10/18/30 During a Physical Reading. 209-1 EC had an unusual dream experience. Upon awakening, he described this experience as follows:

I was preparing to give a reading. As I went out, I realized that I had contacted Death, as a personality, as an individual, or as a being. Realizing this, I remarked to Death: "You are not as ordinarily pictured—with a black mask or hood, or as a skeleton, or like Father Time with a sickle. Instead, you are fair, rose-cheeked, robust—and you have a pair of shears or scissors." In fact, I had to look twice at the feet or limbs, or even at the body, to see it take shape.

He replied: "Yes, Death is not what many seem to think. It is not the horrible thing which is often pictured. Just a change—just a visit. The shears or scissors are indeed the implements most representative of life and death to man. These indeed, unite by dividing—and divide by uniting. The cord does not, as usually thought, extend from the center—but is broken, from the head, the forehead—that soft portion we see pulsate in the infant. Hence we see old people, unbeknowing to themselves, gain strength from youth by kissing there; and youth gains wisdom by such kisses.

Indeed the vibrations may be raised to such an extent as to rekindle or re-connect the cord, even as the Master did with the son of the widow of Nain. For He did not take him by the hand (which was bound to the body as was the custom of the day), but rather stroked him on the head—and the body took life of Life itself! So, you see, the silver cord may be broke—but vibration . . . " Here the dream ended.

Editor's Note: When is one ready for dreams of those who have passed on?

"In commenting on hundreds of such dreams," says Bro, "Cayce offered a number of answers [to this question]:

1. First of all, one is ready for such dreams when he has

them. His subconscious will not feed him experiences he can't handle if he chooses to do so.

2.   Secondly, one is ready for dream contact with the dead when he will not speak lightly of them. In Cayce's view, such dreams could mean dangerous escapism.

3.   Thirdly, one is ready for dreams of the dead when he soundly loves and serves the living; such dreams always come for a personal reason, a personal growth of the dreamer, or some concrete service in the regular round of his daily life. Dream messages seeming to come for a general public are immediately suspect, for healthy contact with the dead was not designed to function for the living in this way.

4.   Fourthly, one is ready for dreams of the dead when he is as ready to give aid to the dead as to receive it. When prayer for a discarnate comes freely and naturally to mind, then visions of them may follow. Any other approach tends to be exploitative.

5.   Fifthly, one is ready for dreams of dead loved ones when he has worked through his griefs and guilts regarding them, and has forgiven them for hurts to himself. Lack of this makes a nearly impenetrable barrier.

6.   Finally, one may dream of the dead when his own full life draws to its natural close, and it is time for him to prepare for the next journey."

6

●

The Dreams of Edgar Cayce

Editor's Note: Having submitted close to one hundred dreams for interpretation, Cayce was himself one of the four people with whom he worked to become "trained dreamers." He undertook the study of his own dreams shortly after he moved to Virginia Beach because he was told to do so by his own readings. Curiously, Cayce would sometimes dream while he was conducting readings in the trance state. Upon awakening, he recollected the dream but recalled nothing concerning the subject of the reading. Once when he submitted a dream for interpretation, his psychic source refused to provide the information because, it said, Edgar Cayce had ignored the lessons of past dream interpretations and done nothing in his life to make correction or adjustment.

Background of Reading 294–196

2/14/40 Early A.M. EC dreamed of talking to his mother, and sought interpretation and lesson to be gained from it, in 294–196.

Reading 294–196

GC: You will have before you the body and the enquiring mind of Edgar Cayce, present in this room, and the dream this body had this morning, February 14, 1940, in which he apparently talked with his mother. You will give the interpretation and lesson to be gained from this.

EC: Yes, we have the body, the enquiring mind, Edgar Cayce, and the dream or vision in which there was the conversation with the mother respecting that idea or thought which has been presented or expressed through the information given many—the return of individual lives; born or reincarnated.

And, as indicated, this is to be a proof to the entity that there is the fact of the rebirth, physically, of an entity or soul; as the mother will, in the nine months, as indicated, be reborn in the earth—and where and among those near and dear to the entity.

This, then, is merely the expression that there may be the thought, the study, the meditation upon the many phases or manners in which the Creative Force—God—works in mysterious ways His wonders to perform among the children of men.

Report of Reading 294–196

GD's note: At time of 294-196 we thought possibly [295]'s expected child was referred to; it was born 11/4/40, a girl, but her Life Reading 2391-1 indicated she had been [4324] in her last incarnation. Interestingly enough, [4324] was a young cousin of EC whom his mother practically brought up; her last name was the same as EC's mother's maiden name, and her given name the same as EC's mother's middle name. She [4324] had died about the same time as EC's mother. [10/13/42 See EC's dream under 294-196 in date sequence, indicating that his mother was still on "the other side" and had not yet been reincarnated.]

Report of Reading 294–196

Editor's Note: The following are uninterpreted dreams that were recorded in this report of Reading 294-196.

2/17/42 Between 11:30 P.M. and 12:30 A.M. of 2/18/42, EC dreamed:

I found myself in the nether land; [world of the dead] recognized it as being along the line I had traveled in going to the house of records to secure Life Readings. Many people I knew were there, both men and women. It seemed as if I had been there for some time. Eventually I met Gertrude and Miss Gladys together. Finally I was able to make myself known to them, and told them we had to go to work; that while this was a place of transition, I was very sure it was also a place of labor. I asked them where they lived. They told me it was along the road. I said, "Well, we've got to build us a place to carry on our work, for the places that are here are what we builded while we were in the earth plane; and while everything comes with just thought, we mustn't just take everything for granted." They answered, "How will we ever build a house—we haven't anything to build it with?" I told them we would first have to find somebody that knew how.

As we were going along, in a very beautiful place, we met someone. I said, "Don't you know who that is?" They each said, "He looks familiar, but I don't know just who it is." I said, "Why, that's Mr. [2051], and he'll build it for us." We all three spoke to him, and eventually were able to make it known to him who we were. But when we told him what we wanted to do, he said, "Oh no, I've got my house, everything I want—why should we have to go to work?" I told him, "Well, we have to work here just as we do anywhere else. If we are just satisfied and sit down here, we'll never get up yonder for Who we are seeking. He may pass this way, but we won't be ready to go anywhere unless we are doing something, and I think we've got a lot to tell these people. It's beautiful, it's lovely, it's quiet; and we don't have to worry about wind or weather or anything to eat, or night or day or anything; because it is whichever one we want—but we must remember that He told us, we must always do everything in decency and in order." So Mr. [2051] said, "Alright, I know some other fellows here—we'll build it." [2/17/42 See 2051-5, Par. R1 in re actual conversation with Mr. [2051] by his daughter on that same night about keeping busy on other side after passing over.] So we went away up the line, this golden line, where it wasn't quite as beautiful in appearance but was still closer to the house of records. He said "I'd like beautiful pine to build it with," and the most beautiful lumber was immediately there—so they put it together; just room after room after room. It all appeared to be finished as soon as put up, almost worked itself. He said, "This is a lot more fun than doing nothing." But he said, "What do you want with so many rooms?" I told him I thought we'd have to carry on the work there. He says, "You going to give Readings here?" I told him maybe I'd have to, because many of those people didn't know who they were, and we don't either, because they've lost their names. And you notice none of us have the same name we did on earth, yet we know who we are. For we have all the one name—*Jesus*. He said, "That's right, I never thought of that. But tell me, have you seen any of these people we expected to see in heaven. Because this is heaven, ain't it?" I told him I didn't know but I thought it was on the right road.

So we began to have meetings in the little house. He'd bring in people and we'd meet people and finally get them to come, for the house was so pretty. There were a great many who couldn't give us any idea of who they were nor what they wanted, and we couldn't tell who they were.

Then as we four were together one time, we saw Dr. House. I told Gertrude and Miss Gladys, "*That's* who we want to help us." So we tried to talk to him. At first he couldn't understand what we were trying to tell him, nor could we make ourselves known to him. But eventually, after recalling to him many things that had happened in earth, he began to recognize us and said he would be glad to commence work again, but he didn't realize people had to work there—that he didn't know as many people as he had thought he would know. So he began to meet with us, and we kept trying to find out for people *who they were, and what they wanted to do!*

Our crowds kept increasing. Then we met, or saw on the road, Dr. Andrew Sargeant—and he was with his first wife, Lizzie Gish. I was the first to recognize them, told Gertrude—she gradually began to recognize them, and then Dr. House recognized him but said he didn't know the woman. So we sent Mr. [2051] and some of those with him to ask them to come to one of our meetings. They came, seemed very happy, but did *not* know why there were attracted to each other. Then I began to tell them *who* they were. Dr. House then suggested, "To get them to understand, why don't you give them a Reading?"

So, for the first time, I laid down and gave a Reading just as I had before, in the earth. All the people gathered about, to listen. Miss Gladys wrote it off on great sheets, it looked like, of cellophane; but as she wrote she realized it was in five different languages—and the English was in the center. There were French and German, Italian and Chinese, and *all* could read. What was given was regarding personal things they did together in the earth, and they recognized it as such. Their question was, "Why were we attracted to each other here, and what must we do about it?" They were told that why they hadn't succeeded was because he wanted children and she did not (while in the earth). Now they would have to have a whole lot of children here, and take care of them, but they were to be the children that hadn't been wanted by parents—or those that had been aborted and there had been sufficient activity for spirit or life to have entered—which they were told occurred at three months.

The house began to grow as they filled the rooms with children. The crowds also began to grow, people also wanting to know who they were. Dr. and Mrs. Sargeant began to keep records of WHO these children were that they took in, and kept them in great files which were light—written in five languages that could be seen as people passed.

I began to wonder how conditions could be improved. And I thought, "What they need in order to know things better is water—water of life, for He said we were to be born of water and of blood." Then I realized there was no bathroom. So I spoke to Mr. [2051] and Dr. House and all the rest, and told them what we were going to do—we were going to ask for the water of life, and we would ask in a Reading whether or not we might have it. As they gathered, Miss Lizzie Gish (Mrs. Sargeant) said, "Now I know what was meant at the meeting when the Lord told you, Mr. Cayce, to 'Teach my people!'" [1/13/40 See EC's dream under 294–189 Reports.]

That's where I woke up. . . .

(Left out—right at the end: Dr. House wanted to know "If Dr. Sargeant working out his failure on earth, now, with his first wife, what must happen to the other two wives he had there?:" So we took a Reading and it said, "They must go back to the earth together, work this out, and then when he meets one of the others and finds out who they are, he'll have to keep the whole thing going in a circle until they have obtained the knowledge—he'll have to work it out with each one.")

12/12/42 P.M. or early Sun A.M. 12/13/42 Edgar Cayce dreamed:
"I was sitting alone in the front room playing solitaire when there

was a knock at the front door. It was dark outside but rather early in the evening. When I went to the door a gentleman whom I did not recognize asked, 'Cayce, I want you to go with me to a meeting this evening.' At first I said 'But I seldom go out of evening and my wife is here and it would leave her alone.' But he insisted I should go with him and I did. As I went out I realized that another person was waiting for us in the street. We walked toward the ocean, but when we came to the ocean we walked on as if into the air, up and up, until we came to where there seemed to be a large circus tent. He said 'We will go in here.' We approached the flap of the tent and as he pulled the flap back, I for the first time, realized that the two men with whom I had been walking were the evangelists Dwight L. Moody and Sam Jones. We entered a large, circular tent; a very unusual kind of light pervaded the place, something like an opalescent light. Many figures were there. All seemed to be shrouded, all dressed alike. Very few I remembered ever having seen before. Then to one side of the place—as more and more figures appeared, until it was full—it seemed that there was a large screen on that side, and as if there was lightening in the distance. With the lightning there was a noise, not of thunder but of wind, yet nothing seemed to stir; and there was no form with the brilliant flashes but as if a cloud, very beautiful. When I asked one of my companions what it was, I was told 'The Lord our God will speak to us.'

"Then a voice clear and strong came as from out of the cloud and the lightning, saying, 'Who will warn my children?' Then from out of the throng before the throne came the *Master*, but as if in the same garb of those about Him. He spoke saying, 'I will warn My brethren.' The answer came back, 'No, the time is not yet fulfilled for you to return, but who shall warn My children?' Then Mr. Moody spoke and said, 'Why not send Cayce, he is there now.'

Then the Master said, 'Father, Cayce will warn My brethren.'

'And we will all help,' came as a grand chorus."

7/10/43 EC wrote Mrs. [3361] that he had recently had the same 12/12/ 42 dream again, or parts of it. "With it has come strength, when seemingly I have not had the strength to go on. Am still a bit dazed, each time the assurance comes, and fearful—like so many of those who have been blessed by His presence and have turned good into selfish purposes and made their people to sin and to forget God.

"Of course I believe in dreams, as so many of those did of old who were called to do some great work—so why shouldn't I? I believe in the God that called Abraham, that spoke to Moses, Joshua, Samuel, David and the God to whom our precious Savior prayed, whom He boldly called 'My Father and your Father.' So what has come to me recently, then, is only an assurance, not something for me to boast of. It is up to me to rely on, and myself *live*, the life of the Savior.

"So, pray with me and for me that I may walk only in the straight and narrow way and present nothing, ever, that Jesus, the Christ, would not sanction at all times.

"Please consider this as sacred as I do, not something to be told to give the impression that I feel I have been called of God above others, or that I have some peculiar hold on the promises of God. For I am sure that all are equal in His sight."

GD's note: In one version of the dream EC made the excuse that he couldn't go because he hadn't finished preparing his Sunday School lesson for the next morning.

In another version the ending was like was this:

"The voice again asked, '*Who will warn my people?*' Then I boldly volunteered, as if I was ready for acceptable. From out of the throng came the Master, Jesus. He blessed me and said, 'I will go with you all the way.'

"Unreal, self-delusionary, you might say. But it has given me a strength, a meekness and, I hope, a kindness that did not exist before.

"No, this is not to be made a religion, a schism or a cult—never! Such experiences are only assurances for myself, not to be told to bring other than the assurance that God is mindful of the children of men."

Reading 294–161

(Q) GC: First, Tues. Morn, Sept. 19th—a copy of which I hold in my hand.

[Dream not read]: I saw myself not as a physical being, but knew that I was part of the whole order of things. Yet, I was only a little snail crawling around on the ground, and recognized that there were many others that were snails also that would eventually be human beings. There were many human beings I didn't know, but I knew they were just occupying different bodies at that time.

Then I saw myself (as the snail) eaten by something else that I had been taught to fear or to expect to be destroyed by.

Then I saw myself as a physical human being, with many human beings who had been snails with me; and many of those who had been human beings were now snails.

I saw myself, as a human being, pass out of the physical body with a fever brought on by eating something which had been infested by the larva of the snail.

Next I recognized myself as a fish swimming in the ocean. There were ships and boats sailing over me. I was able then to communicate with other fish that were of the same variety as myself. Here I saw only very few of the people with whom I had been associated as a physical body. I saw many of my own kind caught in nets, and hooks that were used by men. Finally I saw myself caught in a net, after following several other fish of my kind. We were taken in an enormous net. I saw myself prepared for food, and gradually lost consciousness.

Again I became a physical being, and associated with many more individuals with whom I had been associated as human beings before. Very few of these people had been with me as a fish. I had to do with a lot of cattle, and came to know that I was among those looked after by David, the king of Israel; though he was a shepherd and not a herdsman. I saw him quite often looking after his sheep; and I was changing into a cow, how I didn't know; I merely recognized that I was a cow. Later I had the experience of knowing the feelings of the mother–cow, as I was a mother myself and had a little calf. The calf was scared by the dog that David had with him tending the sheep, which disturbed me (as a cow) very much. I saw him save the calf and bring it back to me for me to take care of, and every time I saw the dog I was enraged at it for trying to harm the calf.

Then I realized I was a dog; didn't know I had died or changed from a cow; but I was a dog and tending the sheep. Then I realized the difference between the dog and the feeling of distrust the dog has for the cows generally, and I saw many cows that had been people I had known.

I seemed to be a very good dog, for I was eventually taken to be in the circus, where I saw many people I had known before as snails, fish, cows and human beings; and I felt the elation of being thought of as a very remarkable and wonderful dog. I had a great desire to make known to all the people my own experience, but could only talk in the dog language. With the number of animals associated in the circus, I recognized the feeling that exists between the cat family and the dog family. Then, in performing one of my acts, in which I had to go through a hoop, I broke my leg; as someone—not intentionally—had misplaced the platform from which I was to jump through a ring (the ring being formed from a grape vine, as the circus was a long time ago and not anything like what we have today). So, I remember very distinctly the man taking a sword (more like a spear) and sticking it through my side, into my heart, to put me out of my misery; which I thanked him for doing.

Again I was a man, and among those guarding the gates in Rome. [Greece? See 294-8 & 294-19 in re Troy] I saw all the fighting, being a guard at the gate. My attendant on the other side of the gate (as the gate opened from the center) I recognized as the one I now know as [5453], but he was much bigger physically than I. I wore a garment that would be called something of a toga today. My trousers were composed of a cloth wrapped around me, gathered and pinned in the middle between my legs. Then another square piece of cloth with a hole for my head dropped over my shoulders. I made armholes in this piece, so that my arms could come through and not have to throw the garment out of the way; which method was afterward adopted by most of the army (or the people, for I didn't recognize them as an army). I saw the battle between Hector and Achilles, recognizing these two as the individuals I now know as [5717] and [900]. They were both beautiful of countenance. Both had matted black ringlets on their heads, which reminded me of Medusa. The hair seemed to be their strength. I noticed that Achilles was very hairy, while Hector only had hair on his neck—which was a different color from the hair on his head. I saw Hector dragged through the gate which I was guarding, into a large arena; and was dragged around the arena several times. Although he was losing, and had lost, quite a bit of blood—leaving the ground and stones bloody as he was dragged along, I noticed that he hadn't wholly lost consciousness. Eventually, the horses—in turning very swiftly, with Achilles driving—caused Hector's head to be dashed against the pillar or the gate near me, and his brains ran out. Before he had even lost the life, or the quiver of the muscles and nerves, I saw the carrion birds eat the great portions of his brain.

Again I passed out, for some reason, and was in the unseen world (from the physical manifestations). I was seeking some way or manner in which I might come back into physical being, and seeking to find others. There were many souls near me who had been in physical bodies, yet very few that I recognized. Finally I did meet someone I had known before, so we decided to come to a mother bird—and we were hatched out by a little jenny wren, as tiny little birds. Then, after we grew up, near the same place where we were hatched out, we built a nest and had a brood of six little birds; then an old cat got them. We were very much distressed, and swore vengeance on the whole cat family.

Then I recognized that I was again manifesting in the material world as a man, very anxious to find the one who had been with me as a little bird the time before. It seemed the time of Columbus' discovering of America, because I was among the people in the land when Columbus came; then I met the individual among the people with Columbus who had been with me as a bird. We were anxious to make a trip on the boat with the people who had come ashore, because we seemed to be the only ones who could talk with them. But we were not allowed to. Then we attempted to get back to the mainland, from the island. A storm came up, and we were drowned.

Next I came into the earth as a man, still in America, at the time of the Civil War. I knew there was a war going on between the north and south country, and that I was in or about the place where I was born in the present. I noticed the home where I was born this time, and the changes—there were more woods then. There were many more people associated with me here that I had known as snails, fish, cows, cats, dogs and sheep—and they were all about me. I started off to see one of the armies where many soldiers were gathered, to find someone I had known before in the various manifestations. Someone told me I had better watch the dogs, cats, and cows that I would meet on the road over which I would go. In going through the great woods I met some of all these, and I could talk in their own language; and I recognized them as being individuals whom I know today. Here I awoke.

(A) EC: Yes, we have the enquiring mind, EC, present in this room, and the dream experience by this body.

Dreams, as indicated, are of different natures; or have their inception from varied causes. In this particular experience or vision may be seen the entity-mind, or soul-mind, seeking—through the varied experiences of the entity—for the kindred thought, that is presented in the emblematical manner of the soul-entity contacting that as is seen of the one force which manifests itself in a material world; and brings—with the activity of that force—an emblematical condition of the mental attributes of a soul.

Hence, in the varied development experienced by the body, there may be seen all forms or characterizations of the result of an influence upon that force that is termed or designated by man as being of one force, or one source, from which all manifested forms may take their activity, as in the relationships of that known as the first law in nature—which is, in an earthly manner, at variance with spiritual law; yet, as experienced by the varied scenes of man's associations with the activities, the result depends upon what the soul of man does about that *it* (the soul) knows concerning the laws, or the *application* of laws, of or toward the first cause; or as to the *purposes* for which that activity comes into being, and the activity's relative position to man's becoming aware *of* the spiritual force in a material world.

Hence, the lesson or the application, is that: The soul of the entity is seeking, through such, to find—as it were—the manners of presenting that which may become Truth, Knowledge, Intellect, or the impulse or impelling influence in the experiences of those who may receive instruction or direction through those channels of associations in the material plane in the present.

Ready for questions.

(Q) *Should this be presented in any literature?*

(A) This is for the entity's or soul, or body's, own interpretation and enlightenment.

For, as seen in the manner in which certain associations were sought, and the environment in which the activity of a soul force sought to know the associations and the understanding of the impelling influence in that termed Nature, or elements, or Life in its manifested varied forms; from the lowest to the highest; and the paralleling of many in the various aspects, as well as seeking out those associations for the relationships that brought the understanding of those propagations in the material activities of an earth's sphere or plane.

Report of Reading 294–161

Editor's Note: The following is an uninterpreted dream that was recorded in this report of Reading 294-161.

2/16/34 Friday a.m. after 2:00 o'clock, Edgar Cayce had the following dream: [5/24/39 EC wrote a version of this dream to Mrs. [1468].]

I was on my way to a camp; had a strap over my shoulder with a little case which reminded me of a case for spy glasses, but I knew I had a message in it that I was to carry to whoever was the commander of the army where I was going. It was rough climbing over the mountain. I came down to the camp very early in the morning; it was just getting light. As I came down into the little ravine I knew there was a stream of water not wider than a person could step over, but I saw a host of men dressed in white; white shoes, trousers, coat and helmet; they each had two straps over their shoulders, one a large canteen–looking container, and they were in groups of four, where they had a fire with a little skillet of some kind over the fire. They made the fire from something they poured out of the canteen; it looked like sawdust, but it was red, green, and brown and might have been ground cork or sawdust. Out of the other can they poured something into the pan, and when they stirred it together it looked like an omelette, or just something good to eat, but I didn't know what it was. I saw no arms, guns, swords or anything of the kind, yet I knew it was an army. I didn't know anyone, but all up and down the ravine I could see the people preparing their breakfast in groups of four. And I asked them where the man in charge was. His tent was farther up or down the ravine. I could see a great white tent in the distance. One here and there joined in showing me the way to go. After a while I came to a place where, over to the right, there was another little ravine that turned off to the right. And as we got just opposite this (myself, and those that had come following me), we heard from out in the darkness someone walking on the sticks; we could hear the sticks break, and we stopped to listen. There appeared a host of people dressed in dark; not dark skin, but their clothing was dark; not black, but dark gray, browns, and the like; all their wrappings were dark.

Then an angel of light stood between us so that we could not see the crowd or group of dark people. Then there appeared the angel of darkness. The angels' figures were very much larger than ours, as men, taller, heavier; of course, their countenance was very much brighter. When the angel of darkness appeared he was dark like the people he was leading, but very much larger. His wings were something like bat wings, yet I knew they were neither feathers nor just flesh, but the means of going fast wherever desired. The wings appeared to be from the loins to the shoulders, rather than just something growing out of the body; both in the angel of darkness and the angel of light. The angel of light had wings something like doves' wings, but extending from the loins to his shoulders, leaving the arms and legs free.

The angel of darkness insisted that he should not stand in the way, but demanded that there be a fight between someone he would choose and one that the angel of darkness would choose. Then there was between the two hosts a place cleared away, something like an arena, and I was chosen as the one to fight with the hosts from darkness. And we were wrestling. I felt that I hadn't delivered my message, and I didn't know just what I would do about it; that I had waited so long and I hadn't told them what I had come for, and I wondered why they had chosen me. I could still feel the strap and little package; I only had the *one* package and wondered why I hadn't been hungry, as the others seemed to have to eat, but I only had the message to carry. Then I began to wonder if my strength was to fail me, if the imp or child of darkness was to put me down in the dirt, it would be an awful thing, but I knew if I could remember one word to say that he couldn't, and I tried and tried to think and couldn't find it; and I couldn't remember what had been written in the message that I was to take.

Finally, as if just from out the center of me, there came the words which I spoke aloud: "And Lo, I am with you always, even unto the end of the world!" As I said that, every one of the darkness fell back and there was a great shout that went up and down the ravine from the people in white. And as they fell back, the leader or angel of darkness (as the one that I was wrestling with fell away) reached out his left hand and struck me on my left hip.

That woke me; and I had an awful pain in my hip.

Bibliography

Bro, Harmon Hartzell. *Edgar Cayce on Dreams: America's Greatest Prophet on How to Understand Dreams—and Make Them Work for You* 1968 (Currently out of print; available on eBay).

Cayce, Hugh Lynn, and Tom C. Clark, Shane Miller, and William N. Peterson. *Dreams: The Language of the Unconscious.* A.R.E. Press, Virginia Beach, VA: 1962 and 1971.

Cayce Readings—the complete readings are available on CD-ROM through the A.R.E.

Sechrist, Elsie. *Dreams: Your Magic Mirror.* A.R.E. Press, Virginia Beach, VA: 1995.

Todeschi, Kevin *Dream Images and Symbols.* A.R.E. Press, Virginia Beach, VA: 1995.

EDGAR CAYCE'S A.R.E.

Who Was Edgar Cayce?
Twentieth Century Psychic and Medical Clairvoyant

Edgar Cayce (pronounced Kay-Cee, 1877-1945) has been called the "sleeping prophet," the "father of holistic medicine," and the most-documented psychic of the 20th century. For more than 40 years of his adult life, Cayce gave psychic "readings" to thousands of seekers while in an unconscious state, diagnosing illnesses and revealing lives lived in the past and prophecies yet to come. But who, exactly, was Edgar Cayce?

Cayce was born on a farm in Hopkinsville, Kentucky, in 1877, and his psychic abilities began to appear as early as his childhood. He was able to see and talk to his late grandfather's spirit, and often played with "imaginary friends" whom he said were spirits on the other side. He also displayed an uncanny ability to memorize the pages of a book simply by sleeping on it. These gifts labeled the young Cayce as strange, but all Cayce really wanted was to help others, especially children.

Later in life, Cayce would find that he had the ability to put himself into a sleep-like state by lying down on a couch, closing his eyes, and folding his hands over his stomach. In this state of relaxation and meditation, he was able to place his mind in contact with all time and space—the universal consciousness, also known as the super-conscious mind. From there, he could respond to questions as broad as, "What are the secrets of the universe?" and "What is my purpose in life?" to as specific as, "What can I do to help my arthritis?" and "How were the pyramids of Egypt built?" His responses to these questions came to be called "readings," and their insights offer practical help and advice to individuals even today.

The majority of Edgar Cayce's readings deal with holistic health and the treatment of illness. Yet, although best known for this material, the sleeping Cayce did not seem to be limited to concerns about the physical body. In fact, in their entirety, the readings discuss an astonishing 10,000 different topics. This vast array of subject matter can be narrowed down into a smaller group of topics that, when compiled together, deal with the following five categories: (1) Health-Related Information; (2) Philosophy and Reincarnation; (3) Dreams and Dream Interpretation; (4) ESP and Psychic Phenomena; and (5) Spiritual Growth, Meditation, and Prayer.

Learn more at EdgarCayce.org.

What Is A.R.E.?

Edgar Cayce founded the non-profit Association for Research and Enlightenment (A.R.E.) in 1931, to explore spirituality, holistic health, intuition, dream interpretation, psychic development, reincarnation, and ancient mysteries—all subjects that frequently came up in the more than 14,000 documented psychic readings given by Cayce.

The Mission of the A.R.E. is to help people transform their lives for the better, through research, education, and application of core concepts found in the Edgar Cayce readings and kindred materials that seek to manifest the love of God and all people and promote the purposefulness of life, the oneness of God, the spiritual nature of humankind, and the connection of body, mind, and spirit.

With an international headquarters in Virginia Beach, Va., a regional headquarters in Houston, regional representatives throughout the U.S., Edgar Cayce Centers in more than thirty countries, and individual members in more than seventy countries, the A.R.E. community is a global network of individuals.

A.R.E. conferences, international tours, camps for children and adults, regional activities, and study groups allow like-minded people to gather for educational and fellowship opportunities worldwide.

A.R.E. offers membership benefits and services that include a quarterly body-mind-spirit member magazine, *Venture Inward*, a member newsletter covering the major topics of the readings, and access to the entire set of readings in an exclusive online database.

Learn more at EdgarCayce.org.

EDGARCAYCE.ORG

Who Was Edgar Cayce?
Twentieth Century Psychic and Medical Clairvoyant

Edgar Cayce (pronounced Kay-Cee, 1877-1945) has been called the "sleeping prophet," the "father of holistic medicine," and the most-documented psychic of the 20th century. For more than 40 years of his adult life, Cayce gave psychic "readings" to thousands of seekers while in an unconscious state, diagnosing illnesses and revealing lives lived in the past and prophecies yet to come. But who, exactly, was Edgar Cayce?

Cayce was born on a farm in Hopkinsville, Kentucky, in 1877, and his psychic abilities began to appear as early as his childhood. He was able to see and talk to his late grandfather's spirit, and often played with "imaginary friends" whom he said were spirits on the other side. He also displayed an uncanny ability to memorize the pages of a book simply by sleeping on it. These gifts labeled the young Cayce as strange, but all Cayce really wanted was to help others, especially children.

Later in life, Cayce would find that he had the ability to put himself into a sleep-like state by lying down on a couch, closing his eyes, and folding his hands over his stomach. In this state of relaxation and meditation, he was able to place his mind in contact with all time and space—the universal consciousness, also known as the super-conscious mind. From there, he could respond to questions as broad as, "What are the secrets of the universe?" and "What is my purpose in life?" to as specific as, "What can I do to help my arthritis?" and "How were the pyramids of Egypt built?" His responses to these questions came to be called "readings," and their insights offer practical help and advice to individuals even today.

The majority of Edgar Cayce's readings deal with holistic health and the treatment of illness. Yet, although best known for this material, the sleeping Cayce did not seem to be limited to concerns about the physical body. In fact, in their entirety, the readings discuss an astonishing 10,000 different topics. This vast array of subject matter can be narrowed down into a smaller group of topics that, when compiled together, deal with the following five categories: (1) Health-Related Information; (2) Philosophy and Reincarnation; (3) Dreams and Dream Interpretation; (4) ESP and Psychic Phenomena; and (5) Spiritual Growth, Meditation, and Prayer.

Learn more at EdgarCayce.org.

What Is A.R.E.?

Edgar Cayce founded the non-profit Association for Research and Enlightenment (A.R.E.) in 1931, to explore spirituality, holistic health, intuition, dream interpretation, psychic development, reincarnation, and ancient mysteries—all subjects that frequently came up in the more than 14,000 documented psychic readings given by Cayce.

The Mission of the A.R.E. is to help people transform their lives for the better, through research, education, and application of core concepts found in the Edgar Cayce readings and kindred materials that seek to manifest the love of God and all people and promote the purposefulness of life, the oneness of God, the spiritual nature of humankind, and the connection of body, mind, and spirit.

With an international headquarters in Virginia Beach, Va., a regional headquarters in Houston, regional representatives throughout the U.S., Edgar Cayce Centers in more than thirty countries, and individual members in more than seventy countries, the A.R.E. community is a global network of individuals.

A.R.E. conferences, international tours, camps for children and adults, regional activities, and study groups allow like-minded people to gather for educational and fellowship opportunities worldwide.

A.R.E. offers membership benefits and services that include a quarterly body-mind-spirit member magazine, *Venture Inward*, a member newsletter covering the major topics of the readings, and access to the entire set of readings in an exclusive online database.

Learn more at EdgarCayce.org.

EDGARCAYCE.ORG